SELLING
SHINE

Lessons Learned by Mastering the
Art of Cleaning and Closing Deals

WILLIAM D. FISHER

Selling Shine:
*Lessons Learned by Mastering the Art of Cleaning
and Closing Deals*

Copyright © 2024 by William D. Fisher

Printed in the United States of America

Paperback ISBN: 978-1-961624-58-0
Ebook ISBN: 978-1-961624-59-7

Canoe Tree
Press

Canoe Tree Press is a division of DartFrog Books
301 S. McDowell St.
Suite 125-1625
Charlotte, NC 28204

www.DartFrogBooks.com

AUTHOR'S NOTE

Dear Reader,

I want to take a moment to share a personal story that has shaped my perspective on life and the importance of giving back to my industry and community.

A few years ago, I was diagnosed with cancer. It was a devastating blow that turned my world upside down. The battle was long and arduous, filled with moments of despair and uncertainty. But through it all, I realized my strong faith in God and discovered the incredible strength of the human spirit and the power of community. My steadfast determination to overcome this obstacle in my life ... support of family and friends ...

During my treatment, I was fortunate to receive support from various cancer organizations. Their unwavering dedication to research, patient care, and raising awareness played a crucial role in my recovery. They provided me with hope, resources, and a sense of belonging in a time of great vulnerability.

Now, as I reflect on my journey, I am filled with gratitude and a deep desire to give back. That is why a portion of the proceeds from this book will be donated to the Jimmy V Foundation for a victory over cancer. By purchasing this book, you are not only investing in your own knowledge and growth but also contributing to the fight against cancer.

Cancer affects millions of lives worldwide, and every contribution, no matter how small, can make a difference. Together, we can support groundbreaking research, provide vital resources to patients and their families, and ultimately work towards a future where cancer is no longer a devastating diagnosis.

I want to express my heartfelt appreciation to you, dear reader, for joining me on this journey and for your support in this endeavor. Together, let us make a positive impact and bring hope to those who need it most.

With gratitude,

William D. Fisher

PROLOGUE

I s the cleaning industry driven by consumerism, where the market saturation with countless products vying for attention, one question remains at the forefront of every business owner's mind: How can I sell my product effectively?

Gone are the days when pricing alone could guarantee success. Today, consumers are more discerning than ever, seeking value beyond just the numbers on a price tag. They crave experiences, solutions, and a connection with the brands they choose to support. In this ever-evolving landscape, the art of selling has transformed into a delicate dance between persuasion, storytelling, and understanding the needs of the modern-day consumer.

This book is not about pricing products; it is about unlocking the secrets to selling them. It delves into the depths of human psychology, exploring the intricate web of emotions, desires, and aspirations that drive purchasing decisions. It reveals the power of effective marketing strategies, captivating storytelling, and building authentic relationships with customers.

Within these pages, you will embark on a journey that will challenge your preconceived notions about selling. You will discover that selling is not merely a transactional exchange but an opportunity to create meaningful connections and to impact lives. Whether you are an aspiring business owner, a seasoned sales professional, or someone simply curious about the art of selling, this book will equip you with the tools and insights to navigate the ever-changing landscape of consumer behavior.

Through real-life examples, case studies, and practical techniques, you will learn how to craft compelling narratives that resonate with your target audience. You will uncover the secrets of effective persuasion, understand the psychology behind decision-making, and leverage the power of emotions to create lasting connections. Moreover, you will gain a deep understanding of the importance of authenticity, trust, and ethical practices in building a successful brand.

But this book is not a magic formula for overnight success. Selling is an art that requires dedication, perseverance, and continuous learning. It is a journey of self-discovery, where you will uncover your unique selling proposition and learn to communicate it effectively. It is a process of trial and error, where you will refine your strategies, adapt to changing trends, and embrace innovation.

So, dear reader, if you are ready to embark on this transformative journey, to unlock the secrets of selling that transcend mere pricing, then turn the page and let the adventure begin. Together, we will explore the depths of human desires, the power of storytelling, and the art of building relationships that will not only sell products but leave a lasting impact on the industry.

TABLE OF CONTENTS

CHAPTER 1

THE KID FROM NEW YORK

I was born and raised in Westbury, New York. My mother worked as a registered nurse, while my father was a salesman in the bustling garment district of downtown Manhattan. Being younger than my siblings, Babs and Bob, our interests often diverged. From an early age, I was exposed to the world of sales through my father. His demeanor at the dinner table was a clear reflection of his day . This early exposure allowed me to develop a deep appreciation for his dedication and work and his unwavering support for our family.

I vividly recall having numerous conversations with my dad about the art of selling. He always advised me to focus on sports, with the aim of securing a college scholarship and eventually turning professional. From an early age, I noticed that my dad frequently entertained his clients, often taking Bob and me along to Knicks and Yankees games. While I enjoyed the spectacle of the games, I was more intrigued by observing how my dad interacted with his customers. In those days, entertainment seemed to be a crucial part of relationship building and customer retention. Interestingly, my dad often referred to the garment business as a 'rat race,' an occupation he deemed unsuitable for his sons.

As I grew up, I immersed myself in sports. Back then, my idols were Mickey Mantle and Thurman Munson in baseball and Walt 'Clyde' Frazier in basketball. As a young boy, I was an advocate for both sports. However, as I matured, I found my true calling in basketball, playing countless two on two games with close friends Bob M. and Bob A. I noticed the parallels between my father's selling skills and the way I displayed my abilities on the basketball court. As I got older, I realized that I was essentially 'selling' my skills to a diverse audience, much like one would market a product to a variety of business sectors today.

At the age of twelve, I dedicated my life to basketball. I quickly understood that I was not going to reach the towering heights of six feet, five inches, so I focused on honing my skills to excel as a point guard. My work ethic was innate, not something acquired. This burning desire to achieve goals and exceed expectations was always within me. Looking back, I am not sure where it originated, but I am grateful for it. I can confidently say that I've put this drive to good use throughout my life.

In 1970, we relocated from New York to Ocean City, New Jersey, a move that required my siblings and me to make significant adjustments. We transitioned from city life to what seemed like a retirement community. My dad's long-term plan was to retire in Ocean City. I remember him commuting via Greyhound bus to Manhattan for several years as we adapted to our new surroundings. He remained committed to his sales job, intending to continue until he felt comfortable enough to retire.

Looking back, it's amusing to note that my dad, who was not athletically inclined, pushed me towards my initial goal of becoming a professional athlete. Interestingly, he later became an avid and highly skilled tennis player. We had numerous conversations about sales, and he always advised me to focus on my sports, assuring me that they would guide me towards my destined path.

Upon moving to Ocean City and being the new kid on the block, I quickly identified areas where I believed I could excel. At that early age, I did not realize that I was essentially 'sizing up the audience,' much like a professional salesperson assesses his customers. I began to excel in basketball and caught the attention of many enthusiasts, earning my place in the sport. I remember spending countless hours on the basketball court, honing my skills, with great friends Naz and Pete. This was my first real commitment to hard work and skill development, lessons that would later prove invaluable in my professional business career. This is why many companies seek to hire former athletes, recognizing their dedication and strong work ethic.

During the summers, I had the opportunity to work on the back of a trash truck, which fit my schedule to play ball all day and into the evening. This unique job came about from the owner of a local trash removal business, who was also a sponsor of our basketball team. It was quite an experience, lifting heavy metal trash cans filled with all sorts of garbage and hoisting them into the compactor. At that time, recycling was not as prevalent, so we had to be cautious of sharp objects. Despite wearing gloves, I still bear the scars from those encounters. As we completed our shifts, my fellow workers and I would often playfully yell at girls heading to the beach, only to receive laughter and dismissive responses. However, amidst the hard work and occasional banter, I had the pleasure of meeting some wonderful people like Sonny and Bobbie. After our early morning shifts, we would gather at a nearby diner where they introduced me to a delicious meal of scrambled eggs topped with creamed chip beef and a side of potatoes with fried onions. I instantly became hooked on this hearty breakfast. My time working on the trash truck taught me the importance of commitment and getting the job done, regardless of the less-than-ideal surroundings. The owner, Pete, ran a tight ship and instilled in us a strong work ethic. I did manage to get a week to break away from working to attend the 5-Star invite only basketball camp, where I caught the eye of some of the top college recruiters.

My team in Ocean City was good, and I emerged as the star player from my sophomore through senior year, averaging twenty-three points per game. An analysis of my game footage revealed that, had the three-point line been in play, I would have averaged an impressive forty points per game. I was known for my long-range shots. However, this experience taught me a valuable lesson: one person alone cannot consistently win games, especially when you are up against a box-in-one most of the time. I came to understand that reaching the pinnacle of any profession requires the support of a dedicated team, each member playing their part to secure consistent victories.

During my high school career, I was courted by numerous major colleges, an experience unlike any I had encountered before. One coach that made a huge impression on me was Jim Valvano, who was coaching at Iona at the time. "Work hard and never give up on your dreams," he said. We played against Iona that year in the holiday classic played at Madison Square Garden. It was a close game, but they came out the victor. It's ironic later in life that we were both stricken with cancer. He made a huge impact on the sport and touched so many people before his death. Other college coaches would visit my home, attempting to persuade my parents and me why their institution was the best fit for me. It was challenging to discern sincerity from mere sales talk. This was the first time I had to critically evaluate my abilities and determine where I would have the best opportunity to quickly advance in college basketball. I chose the University of South Florida in Tampa, a division one school with one of the best schedules in the country.

I embarked on five recruiting trips to various colleges in the summer of 1976. The most amusing, yet sincere, approach was from my future coach. He arranged for a group of attractive young women in to casually stroll past his office window during our meeting. Later, when I got to know him better, I asked him about this tactic. He laughed and admitted, "Those were my selling props. They worked, didn't they? I got you here, didn't I?"

The first year at South Florida was a typical adjustment period that most students experience when they go away to college for the first time. However, the drinking and partying scene in Florida seemed more intense than what I had anticipated compared to other colleges. It was a temptation that was difficult to resist, but I made a conscious effort to keep it under control, and I did a decent job. As a first-year student, I performed well coming off the bench and had the opportunity to compete against some of the finest basketball players in college, such as Phil Ford and Walter Davis from North Carolina, Ernie and Bernie from Tennessee, and the Running Rebels from Las Vegas, among others. The recruiting process did not stop, as I received another scholarship offer from a coach who had previously missed recruiting me to his former school. He was now at Mississippi State University and believed I would be the perfect fit as their point guard. So, here I was, a kid from New York, making the decision to venture into what is considered the Deep South in Mississippi.

I remember my mom accompanying me to help me settle in, just like many families do when their kids go off to college. My parents believed that this transition would be a significant adjustment, which is why my mom came along. To my surprise, the athletic director approached us and requested a meeting. Since I had been there for two weeks before my mom arrived, she turned to me and asked, "What on earth did you do?" I honestly had no idea what he wanted to discuss. During the meeting, he asked if it was all right for me to room with a black student athlete, as they had never done that before. My mom and I exchanged surprised glances and assured him that I had many black friends and would be honored to room with him. This incident occurred in 1978, and I was shocked to witness how far behind they were in terms of eliminating racial biases from their mindset.

I gained an ardent appreciation for the role of a point guard in the SEC. As a point guard, you are responsible for bringing the ball up, setting up the offense, and playing stellar defense. While that style of play was not exactly my forte, I did my best to adapt. Unfortunately, during my time at Mississippi State, I did not have the opportunity to fully highlight my skills as I had anticipated. I mostly came off the bench. However, what I will always cherish is the strong bond formed with my teammates, who came from diverse backgrounds but shared the same aspirations of playing professional sports. Little did we know at that time that the chances of making it to the professional level in basketball were only around 2 percent. I strongly believe that coaches should have open conversations with their players, informing them about the realities they may face in life. Many athletes are unaware of the challenges and the slim chances of getting paid to play professionally, which are not as easy as they may appear.

I recall one morning when my marketing professor asked me to join him for a cup of coffee. During our conversation, he delivered a message that would have a lasting impact on my life: I was not going to become a professional basketball player. This revelation hit me hard, but it also opened my eyes to the multitude of other professions where I could find success and build a fulfilling, long-lasting career. I looked at him, eager for guidance, and asked how I should proceed. His response was simple yet profound: I needed to prioritize my education by attending classes and dedicating the same level of effort I had put into basketball over the years. He emphasized that obtaining a college degree was my first step. Additionally, he encouraged me to explore my interests and identify my strengths. He explained that many individuals find themselves in lucrative jobs that leave them unhappy, highlighting the importance of finding a career that aligns with one's passions. He stressed that since a sizable portion of our lives is spent at work, it is crucial to pursue something we genuinely enjoy, as it will reward our hard work with both personal fulfillment and financial gain. I owe a great deal to that marketing professor, as his guidance set me on the right path and propelled me forward in life.

I underwent a noticeable transformation within myself. I began to genuinely enjoy my studies and found myself immersed in the learning process. It became a running joke on campus: "Have you seen Bill Fisher in the library? I have never seen him there before!" Little did they know that I would soon become a regular fixture, spending countless hours in the library, diligently catching up on the coursework I had neglected during my first two years on campus. I started collaborating with a group of highly intelligent students, and although I may not have been the smartest among them, I excelled in leading projects and earned the respect of my peers off the basketball court. My commitment to graduating on time was unwavering, even if it meant enduring the sweltering heat of two summer school sessions to make up for lost time. Reflecting, I now realize that in basketball, you are constantly selling yourself to your coach, the fans, the alumni, and even your competitors. I had not fully grasped this concept at the time, but looking back, I see the various facets of self-promotion involved. Unfortunately, it seems that many athletes overlook this aspect and fail to appreciate how integral selling oneself is to their overall autonomy.

On the journey back to New Jersey, I recognized that my basketball journey was far from over. Having dedicated my life to the sport, I felt compelled to give it one last shot and see if I could capture the attention of professional recruiters and scouts. I had heard about The Baker League, a renowned summer pro league in Philadelphia, and decided to pack my gear and attend the open tryouts. To my surprise, I outperformed the other point guards, many of whom had been previously drafted. My coach for the league was the legendary Sonny Hill, who had made a tremendous impact on the basketball community in the Philadelphia area through his sponsorship of various basketball leagues and charities. I was assigned to the team called Bubble Car Wash, alongside talented teammates such as Joe Bryant, Mel Bennett, Mike Bantom, and the exceptional Lloyd Free. Throughout the league, I opened the eyes of numerous seasoned professionals, hoping that someone would take notice and give me a chance. Our team emerged victorious in the league conference, and I walked away from the experience with a newfound confidence, knowing that I belonged among the elite. To provide some context, I had the privilege of knowing Joe Bryant and his wife even before the birth of their son, Kobe. The rest is history. The basketball community is a tight-knit group of individuals who share a deep love for the game.

Lessons Learned

- Take time to appreciate your past, as there will always be a desire for more or a feeling that you could have done more. Allow yourself to reminisce and find joy in your accomplishments.

- If your parents are still alive, hug them for everything they did for you.

- Choose your profession and pursue it with determination.

- Embrace failure as a learning opportunity, gather your strength, brush off the setbacks, and relentlessly pursue your dreams.

- Outwork everyone!

CHAPTER 2

HOOP DREAMS SHATTERED
BUT NOT IN THE BUSINESS WORLD

Reality hit me hard when I came to terms with the fact that my dreams of playing professional basketball would never materialize. I had to say good-bye to my dream of playing in the NBA and figure out what I would do for the rest of my life. Considering this realization, I decided to take on a part-time job at a liquor store owned by a friend. Simultaneously, I began scouring the want ads for job opportunities. Sales positions were in high demand back then, particularly at esteemed companies like IBM, 3M, and New York Life. However, I encountered a significant hurdle–these prestigious companies all required prior sales experience, which I lacked. Despite my efforts, I struggled to make headway in pursuing sales opportunities with these top-tier organizations. Then, one day in the summer of 1980, I stumbled upon an advertisement that seemed almost ironic in today's business world. The ad sought out a ambitious young salesman to replace an aging salesforce. It immediately caught my attention, as it aligned perfectly with my skill set. I called the owner, who invited me to visit on a Saturday morning. At the time, I was dating a girl from Philadelphia, and she asked if she could accompany me.

I agreed, and as we approached the warehouse, I understood it was situated in a rough neighborhood. However, having played basketball on those very courts for many years, I did not perceive it as a dangerous area. As we pulled up to the warehouse, she noticed a bullet hole through the glass of the office and turned to me, expressing her disbelief, questioning whether I would work there. I assured her that she could take the car, as we did not have cell phones back then, and instructed her to return in about an hour to pick me up. This confidence instilled in me initially by Ben set a profound appreciation for wholesale distribution, as you will discover later in the book. It was common for janitorial supply wholesale distributors to be in run-down areas. However, I quickly realized that the location of a facility has no bearing on one's ability to effectively serve customers.

I walked into Ben's office, and our conversation remains etched in my memory as if it happened yesterday. He asked if I was married, to which I replied with a simple "no." Then he inquired about having a girlfriend, and I confirmed that I did. Ben proceeded to share a valuable piece of advice that has stuck with me ever since. He said, "If your girlfriend can't handle it when you're at a party and someone asks about your profession, and you can't confidently look them in the eye and proudly say, 'I sell toilet tissue,' then you're going to encounter problems." He emphasized that it is not about what you sell, but rather how you represent yourself and your company, and how effectively you persuade people to buy based on the value you provide. He added, "Kid, you can make a lot of money selling toilet paper. So, who cares what you sell if you are successful and making a good living?" He continued, offering me a starting salary of $11k, but assured me that with hard work, I could potentially earn $70-80k within a couple of years. At the time, I was only twenty years old, and without hesitation, I eagerly accepted the offer.

In today's world, it is rare to find someone juggling two jobs at the same time. It makes me wonder whatever happened to those principles of hard work and determination. In the following anecdotes, I hope you find humor and enjoyment as I recount my experiences from both jobs. Each of these experiences is intertwined with the art of selling and the pursuit of earning an income, both during the day and at night.

My Day Job

Initially, my focus at the wholesale distributor was on learning the administrative side of the business before venturing into the field. I remember receiving a book that contained information about all our products, with the pricing details tucked away in a side folder. The approach was to throw the book at you and expect you to learn through trial and error. Although it was a challenging method, it was the only way to succeed if you were truly determined. Additionally, it was fascinating to observe the diverse training dynamics, where the manufacturers took a keen interest in ensuring that we had a solid understanding of the product line. As you progressed through the book, you noticed a significant shift in training responsibilities.

I quickly learned how to effectively utilize my time with manufacturers' representatives and fill their fieldwork schedule. All I had to do was spark the interest of potential customers and arrange workdays with the manufacturers. This allowed me to witness their sales pitch and receive on-the-fly training. I would assess what I perceived as weak and eliminate it from my own approach. Additionally, I always paid close attention to the body language and expressions of the customers.

Collaborating with my sales colleagues was both fascinating and fulfilling. I have vivid memories of conducting business with custodians at the bar, a practice that would be deemed unacceptable in today's culture. The experienced representative I was shadowing enlightened me about the concept of having "all of the power lines," a term I heard for the first time. This referred to the secret sauce of building margin and commissions. During that era, the distribution industry was not overly saturated, so manufacturers established relationships on a semi-exclusive or exclusive basis to safeguard the distributor's margins. In the sanitary maintenance industry of the 1980s, some of these power lines included Scott Paper, Johnson's Wax, Clark, 3M, and Triple-S, among others.

The Scott Paper representatives had a distinct style and approached business in a unique manner. They always presented themselves in a professional manner, with polished shoes and a professional demeanor. They understood the importance of dressing for success and making a lasting first impression. Selling a high-quality brand of paper, they knew how to effectively justify the higher cost of their product. From the very beginning, I received hands-on training in selling a premium brand and explaining the value to justify the price. Simply put, they entered customer meetings with an air of professionalism that was immediately noticed by the customers. Without even uttering a word, they had already earned initial respect. Their representatives were exceptionally knowledgeable about their products, well-versed in their competition, and possessed the ability to guide customers through the sales process, ensuring they made informed decisions when purchasing quality products.

Johnson's Wax was the leading chemical line in the industry and a must-have for wholesale distributors. The brand carried significant weight due to its proven products. When it came to innovation and new product development in the floor-care industry, Johnson's Wax was unparalleled. One of their standout products was Complete floor finish, which they marketed exceptionally well. It became highly sought after by everyone. Unlike consumables, floor-care systems required preparing and recoating of floors, and Johnson's Wax represented a line that offered more speed and durability. They were trendsetters with their J-Shop project, which focused on bulk chemicals. This unique delivery system set the stage for my first major account opportunity with Ciba-Geigy, a manufacturer of dyes, pigments, resins, and epoxy additives in the Tom's River area.

Initially, it was a cold call that turned into a valuable learning experience for me and opened doors for future opportunities in my career. I requested a meeting with the head of operations and the head of purchasing. While the head of operations was typically off-limits, I was fortunate enough to sit down with the purchasing manager and gain valuable insights. I always began by asking how they preferred to conduct business and what protocols to follow. This approach established a level of confidence in my abilities and helped to open doors. My second question focused on the number of vendors currently servicing their account. I quickly learned that by assessing the competition, highlighting potential savings through simplification, and identifying areas for cost reduction within the plant, I could make a significant impact.

Lastly, I inquired about whether the operations manager's budget was tied to cleaning products. As a professional sales representative, it was important to find the most efficient route to participate in the company's cost reduction meetings as a trusted advisor.

During the conversation, I discovered that they had four existing vendors, all of which were large paper companies from Philadelphia and New York. I then asked the purchasing manager about his biggest pain point, and he mentioned their central receiving warehouse, which was overflowing, and the challenges of delivering cleaning products to various buildings. I seized the opportunity and presented a solution. I explained that we had a bulk chemical program with onsite replenishment tanks that could alleviate some of the issues associated with transporting pallets of chemicals. Furthermore, I proposed the idea of implementing scheduled replenishment for these bulk tanks to streamline the delivery, as well as adding all associated products.

The purchasing manager expressed interest in knowing the price per gallon for the degreaser, which was used in various production areas on the floor. Recognizing that I had a clear advantage over their current supplier, I was able to easily calculate the potential savings right in front of him. Curious about their annual usage, I asked how many gallons they typically went through and his cost per gallon. To my surprise, he provided me with the information. I shifted my notepad towards him and as he saw the cost savings, he was astonished. In fact, he uttered a sentence that proved invaluable: "This one product's savings will contribute 30 percent to my overall cost-saving goal for the year." He immediately expressed his intention to set up a test with the operations department, and upon their approval, we would determine the timing for transition, the number of bulk tanks required, their placement, and schedule shipments.

This experience taught me a valuable lesson-by uncovering the true needs of potential customers and providing solutions, you can enhance your value and differentiate yourself from competitors. It was interesting to observe that when I was on-site with the operations manager, he had more time to spend with me. This allowed me to gain his confidence and support in transitioning other products from my company. As a result, the purchasing manager was able to reduce his vendor base and simplify his business operations. Eventually, they became one of our largest accounts. This success served as a reference point when approaching new industrial customers, demonstrating the value and benefits they could achieve by collaborating with us.

In sales, it is pivotal to be willing to knock on new doors, handle rejection, and expand your customer base. By doing so, you can establish new connections and build your book of business. Networking and forming relationships with customers like this have proven to be invaluable.

The Clarke Floor Machine company was our primary equipment line, we had an equipment van and an experienced specialist named Ray. Ray was an asset to the company, handling equipment sales, service, and various other tasks around the warehouse. One day, I approached Ray and asked if I could ride along with him for an equipment demonstration. I remember sitting in the van as we drove what felt like an eternity to the late evening demonstration at a plant. We had to sign in at the security desk and then proceed to the pre-assigned area to set up the machine for the demonstration.

During that time, Clarke's main competitor was Advance. Unlike today, where there are multiple competitors in the industry, back then we only had a few direct competitors. Learning and selling equipment was a unique experience that would become a significant part of my career. Ray taught me a valuable lesson about testing the machines to ensure they were fully operational. Selling maintenance equipment involved various costs, including demo equipment, transportation of the machines, selecting the demo location, and the time required to travel from point *A* to *B* and conduct the on-site demonstration.

Curious about price sensitivity, I asked Ray if the equipment could be discounted. He explained that due to the associated expenses, discounting was not feasible. Instead, he advised me to focus on highlighting the four-to-five key features that differentiated our equipment from competitors. By preempting the competitor and highlighting our machine's unique capabilities, we could make a strong impression. Ray's approach to the demonstration was simple yet effective: wow the audience in the first five minutes with the machine's floor performance, and then place it in the hands of the operators. He emphasized the importance of never leaving their side, as they could become our enthusiastic advocates and influence the decision to choose our machine.

Ray's approach worked so well that the customers decided to purchase the machine on the spot. As Ray humbly put it, "We may have been the last to demo, but we got the order, that's what counts."

Recognizing my early success and eagerness to further develop my skills, Ben decided to send me to the highly sought-after Clarke training school. It was there that I had the privilege of meeting Dwayne, who had been Clarke's sales trainer for many years. Without a doubt, Dwayne was the best sales trainer I have encountered throughout my forty-two-year career. His demeanor exuded a deep knowledge of the products and the industry, and he made it a priority to impart as much of that knowledge as possible during the week of training. Dwayne took the time to personally connect with each sales attendee, ensuring that his training resonated with all of us. There are certain individuals whose impact on your career remains etched in your memory, and for me, Dwayne is one of them. I distinctly remember him always carrying a cigarette holder, a simple yet unforgettable detail. I often wondered if it were a prop or if he simply could not wait to step outside for a smoke break.

After completing the week of training, Dwayne drove the van that dropped us off at the airport. As we parted ways, he turned to me and said, "Bill, go out there and sell some damn Clarke for me." Inspired by his words, I returned to my company with a newfound determination to seek out opportunities to sell Clarke equipment. With Ray and the local Clarke equipment representative by my side, I felt confident in pursuing equipment deals. I had learned how to identify potential opportunities and had developed a newfound confidence in selling capital goods. However, my heavy focus on selling Clarke equipment meant that I had to dedicate more time to my sales role, making it increasingly challenging to continue working my night job at the liquor store.

At that time, 3M stood out as the most innovative company in the sanitary maintenance industry. Their sales representatives were highly trained and carried themselves with the same aura that I mentioned earlier regarding the

Scott Paper representatives. With their customary blue suits, red ties, and high-quality branded products, they commanded respect when entering customer meetings. Larry, the 3M sales representative for our account, was incredibly helpful to me in the initial stages. He took the time to guide me in the right direction for expanding our portfolio. 3M had a wealth of marketing information that opened my eyes to new industries and the products that could help us enter those markets.

Drawing on my strengths, I focused on setting up introductory meetings with potential buyers. I made sure to have all relevant stakeholders present during these meetings to ensure productivity. It was imperative to have everyone at the customer's level in attendance, as this maximized our time and shortened the sales cycle. I became adept at opening doors, scheduling meetings, and positioning the close. Prior to each meeting, I would gather pertinent information by asking questions, briefing Larry so that he was up to speed on the attendees and their pain points. This allowed us to strategize our approach effectively. I learned a great deal from Larry during his sales presentations, and there was one conversation that has always stuck with me. I expressed to Larry that I believed I was better at selling his products than he was. In response, Larry looked at me and said, "Young man my job is done here. You don't need me anymore." He had mastered his craft and knew that I would now be carrying the 3M flag. In that moment, he effectively added another member to his platoon of distributor sales reps.

In the early days, I observed a geographical expansion among manufacturers in the sanitary maintenance industry. This led to overlapping distribution and multiple representatives carrying the same product lines, resulting in competition for the same customers. To address this challenge and protect profit margins, the concept of private labeling emerged. Ben played an active role in the development of the first association in the industry, known as Triple-S. Attending Triple-S meetings holds many cherished memories for me. The association consisted of premier distributors across the country who collaborated on private labeling to safeguard their businesses and accounts. It served as a valuable resource on a national level, and throughout my career, I have maintained a close connection with this association and formed lasting friendships with individuals who have supported me along the way.

I distinctly recall the significant presence of Rubbermaid in the school business, with truckloads of their products being delivered to schools. Back then, investing in Rubbermaid products yielded a good return. While Continental was a rival, their products did not match the quality or brand recognition that Rubbermaid had established in the industry.

I recall Ben's excitement when we received the news that Atlantic City would be getting casinos. It felt like we had hit the jackpot. I had numerous discussions with him about the major companies in New York and Philadelphia that would undoubtedly flock to this new landscape. I believed that while they were busy competing for what would be lower-margin business in Atlantic City, we should focus on expanding into the Philadelphia market. Ben took my advice and acquired a company in Pennsauken, just outside of Philadelphia. This move transformed me into a working sales manager, responsible for developing a younger salesforce in both locations as our older representatives approached retirement. Transitioning from a sales role to a management position is a momentous change for most sales reps. Some adapt and excel, while others struggle with the shift. It is because saying "no" becomes a necessary part of the job, and sales reps typically dislike hearing that word. Drawing from the experience I had gained, I decided to take a page from Larry's playbook and build my own team of dedicated sales representatives.

During my early years in the industry, I surrounded myself with a group of professionals who helped me quickly grasp the intricacies of the business and the multitude of opportunities within the industry. It was truly the golden era of displaying and selling products. I can distinctly recall that I never went out into the field without something in my vehicle to demonstrate. It was a form of forced learning, and I learned not to be afraid of failure. It was remarkable how many customers were willing to support a young individual like me in succeeding. For those who took an interest in me and offered their guidance, it left an indelible mark on my life and career. I am forever grateful for those cherished moments.

My Night Job

Growing up in Ocean City, New Jersey, there was a distinct difference compared to most places-the city had been dry for as long as I can remember. To purchase any alcohol, one had to cross either the Ninth Street Bridge or the Thirty-third Street Bridge to reach a liquor store. This resulted in massive crowds and heavy traffic during the summer months as people flocked to these stores. The liquor store I worked at was called Boulevard Liquors, owned by two brothers named Dave and Dan. Dave and I played basketball together on many occasions, while Dan was heavily involved in politics.

The team I worked with at the liquor store consisted of a mix of teachers and athletes. It was a diverse group that worked harmoniously and enjoyed the constant surprises brought by customers seeking their favorite drinks.

My role at the store involved working at the counters and in the cold box, where we stored refrigerated beverages. What I enjoyed most about working at the counter was interacting with the different customers and experiencing their unique personalities. During that time, we did not have scanning systems, so it was our responsibility to manually put price tags on each bottle when the liquor arrived. It is amazing to see how technology has advanced today, with scanning and inventory controls in grocery and liquor stores. Nowadays, there are even delivery services for alcoholic beverages, a convenience that many people take advantage of. You do not even have to leave your house to get your favorite drinks anymore.

Working at the liquor store provided me with an opportunity to study facial recognition, body language, and dispute resolution. I encountered various experiences during evenings and weekends. The crowds that frequented the store were often referred to as "shoobies," as they were visitors from Philadelphia or summer homeowners who were not permanent residents of the city. As a result, they sometimes came with a bit of an attitude.

One aspect of my job that I found interesting was dealing with underage individuals attempting to purchase alcohol. It was amusing to observe them nervously picking up items for their friends and then approaching the counter to see if they would get lucky and go unnoticed. However, we always asked for ID, and upon inspection, we would often discover their attempts at forging identification. I even went as far as challenging them to convince me why they should be allowed to purchase the liquor, which led to some hilarious responses. Nowadays, everyone is required to show identification before purchasing alcohol, but back then, we primarily carded younger individuals who were on the verge of being underage. We were aware of the fines associated with serving underage customers and were diligent in upholding our responsibilities.

Occasionally, we encountered customers attempting to shoplift. They were easy to spot, especially during the sizzling summer days when they would come into the store wearing hoodies or carrying backpacks, trying to act cool, calm, and collected. We were vigilant in checking for any signs of shoplifting. While we never prosecuted anyone, we made it clear that they were not welcome back into the store.

Another aspect of our job was dealing with intoxicated individuals. We would often notice them stumbling before they even reached the counter, and we were concerned about their safety. In most cases, we would kindly ask them to leave, and in some instances, we would call a cab to ensure they got home safely.

Teamwork and Unity

One of the highlights of each shift was the camaraderie we shared with our team and the owners. After the store closed, we would gather, have a few beers, and reminisce about our experiences, sharing laughter and appreciating one another's company.

Whenever we encountered a problem that we could not manage on our own, such as a group of threatening individuals, we would simply pick up the phone and call the two brothers who owned the store. Both were imposing figures, standing at six feet, five inches, and weighing over two hundred and fifty pounds each. Their presence alone was enough to make troublemakers think twice and quickly leave the premises.

Another aspect of the job that I observed was the loyalty between the store owners and the liquor salesmen who called on them. Despite the possibility of other distributors offering cheaper prices on certain items, Dave and Dan remained loyal to the representatives who had helped them build their business. The long-term friendships and partnerships between them were evident, and they valued the support and influence these reps had in ensuring that the store shelves were always well stocked.

This experience taught me that loyalty can take various forms. In this case, it was the longevity of the relationships between the store owners and the sales representatives. It would be interesting to know the number of times these reps responded to emergency needs and how efficiently those needs were met.

Working at the liquor store provided me with a unique perspective on life. Unfortunately, later in life, I experienced the loss of my brother at the age of sixty-six due to alcoholism. It is a devastating habit and addiction that affects many individuals. My advice to anyone struggling with uncontrollable urges is to reach out for help. There are numerous organizations and individuals who have gone through similar addictions and are dedicated to assisting others in finding the right path. I have personally helped several people overcome their addiction, but it remains a source of sadness that I could not convince my brother to get help.

Lessons Learned

- If you are driven and can hone your skills, you have the potential to sell anything and make a great living.
- Discover the sales approach that suits you the best, discard any other methods, and if it proves successful, build upon it. If it doesn't yield results, either fix it or consider exploring other career options outside sales.
- Break out of your shell and embrace the challenges of cold calling.
- On every sales call, prioritize adding value. If you fail to do so, you may find yourself losing on price.
- Make time and appreciate the relationships you have with family and friends.

CHAPTER 3

RECOGNIZING IMPACT COMPANIES

In late 1987, I was introduced to Windsor, a carpet cleaning manufacturer, and was impressed by their culture and innovative products, which I believed would be phenomenally successful in the sanitary maintenance industry. Intrigued, I expressed my interest in learning more about the company to Paul, their national sales manager at the time. Paul informed me about an opening in the Metro New York market and arranged an interview with Charlie, the executive vice president, at their manufacturing plant in Englewood, Colorado. Prior to my visit, Paul suggested that I invest in a pair of Florsheim Imperial wingtip shoes, as Charlie had a fondness for them, and it would make a good first impression during the interview. Following his advice, I purchased a $200 pair of shoes and arrived fully prepared for the interview. As I entered Charlie's office and we were introduced, we shook hands and he immediately glanced at my shoes with a slight grin, remarking that he liked me already because of the wingtips. The interview began with a discussion about my family, faith, and industry experience, in that order, before moving on to the topic of the New York metropolitan territory.

The New York territory market was being managed by an individual who was not well-liked by distributors. Kevin was a good guy, just in a market that demanded more of his time. I understood that establishing an unknown brand in the market could be challenging, and sometimes people react negatively under pressure instead of positively. Unfortunately, the territory was not generating the desired volume of sales that Charlie and Paul had hoped for in the large metropolitan New York market.

Curious about the current performance of the territory, I asked Paul about its sales. He informed me that it was approximately $300,000. Charlie then inquired about my current income and commission program with my current employer. I explained that I had a salary of $70,000, with an additional $20,000 in commission. I also enjoyed benefits such as a company car and an expense account. Charlie proceeded to explain their typical commission program for independent reps, which consisted of a 10 percent commission and a 3 percent quarterly bonus for reaching sales goals. However, recognizing that this would be a challenging project, they were willing to offer me a 15 percent commission and the 3 percent quarterly bonus for the first year if I achieved my targets.

Quickly assessing the opportunity, I realized that I could potentially take the $300,000 territory to $1 million in sales. Based on my calculations, that would amount to $180,000 in commission. I pointed out to Charlie that their offer, considering the current revenue of the territory, would only be around $52,000, and I would cover my own expenses. I also mentioned that I lived in South Jersey, which was two and a half hours away from the territory. Charlie expressed concern that a sizable portion of my commissions would be eaten up by expenses such as lodging, gas, and other costs associated with running an independent rep organization. **Charlie must have seen my grit and determination.** I confidently replied that I would take the offer.

To their surprise, Charlie and Paul exchanged glances and welcomed me to Windsor. Charlie became my first mentor in my career, and we developed a close friendship until his passing at the age of ninety-four. He was a legend in the industry and had a wealth of experience, which I always sought to tap into whenever possible. Charlie was always intrigued by my quick decision-making. He would ask me repeatedly, "What were you thinking?" I would respond by saying that while they were considering the $64,800 with a modest 20 percent increase, I had already envisioned earning $180,000. I was determined to do everything in my power to achieve that goal. This mindset marked the beginning of my approach to go backwards to make significant strides forward in my career. Unlike most people in business who expect more when changing positions, I was different. I was not concerned about making more money; I knew I would reach that point quickly. I always had confidence in my abilities to earn more as I progressed in my business career.

After I accepted the job, it was time to lay the groundwork for achieving my goal of earning $180,000. I began by mapping out the distribution channels and conducting research on the distributors and distributor sales reps (DSRs). It was crucial for me to identify the reps with larger books of business who could immediately introduce me to their premier accounts, allowing me to display our equipment and secure sales. I dedicated a massive portion of the week to developing action plans and determining the necessary steps to elevate our brand in the Metro New York market. Additionally, I focused on aligning with the right distribution partners to ensure a favorable return on my time investment. I was advised that by monetizing every aspect associated with "the sale," I could gain a true understanding of my return on time.

This opportunity marked my first venture into independent representation. At twenty-seven years old, I felt confident about starting my own company, one where I had complete control and could rely on my strong work ethic to achieve the goals I had set for myself. My selling philosophy was straightforward: if I were not the smartest or most experienced, I would simply outwork and outlast my competitors. I believed that by working harder than them, they would eventually make mistakes, allowing me to surpass them and emerge victorious in the market.

As I delved into the expenses involved, I quickly realized that I was in a challenging financial situation. Brenda was pregnant with our first baby, we had just purchased a house, and she was understandably concerned about my decision. However, I reassured her that I had everything under control and confidently declared that we would achieve financial freedom within the next nine months. In fact, I intentionally shortened my goal from twelve months to nine months to reach the million-dollar mark. This approach of setting shorter timeline goals is something salespeople should consider, as it puts pressure on oneself to achieve targets within a condensed period. This strategy helps to ensure that one stays on track, even when faced with unforeseen circumstances.

One of the major expenses I had to consider was investing in a full-size van to transport the demonstration equipment. It was crucial for me to be fully prepared and able to demonstrate a variety of equipment to each potential customer. Additionally, I factored in the costs of insurance for the van and all the associated expenses that come with maintaining a working vehicle. Fuel costs were also a significant consideration.

Fortunately, my wife worked as a medical technologist and had excellent health benefits through the hospital she was employed with. This alleviated the need for additional expenses related to health coverage on our profit and loss statement.

As I made my way up the toll-ridden Garden State Parkway, I knew I needed to find a place to live and establish a home base. I decided on Parsippany, New Jersey, as it provided a direct route into Manhattan. I stopped by the Red Roof Inn, where the nightly rates were initially $115. However, I negotiated with the manager, proposing that if I committed to staying three to four nights a week, could they reduce the rate by half. Eventually, we settled on $55 per night, and the Red Roof Inn became my regular accommodation. Although most days I would leave by 5:00 a.m. in the morning, there were occasions when I had a later start. On those days, I would leisurely come down to the office in my robe, greet everyone, grab a cup of coffee, a newspaper, and head back to my room.

In addition to lodging expenses, I had to consider other costs such as meals and tolls on the Garden State Parkway, New Jersey Turnpike, and the tunnels or bridges when traveling in and out of the city. Each trip through these routes incurred a $5 fee.

To pick up my demo machines, I visited a distributor in Brooklyn owned by David. The machines were stored in his garage, and upon inspection, I noticed they were worn out and heavily used. I vividly remember opening the hood of the box extractor and discovering a residential water faucet used as a substitute for the solution valve. I knew this would present some challenges, but I refused to let it deflate me right from the start. Instead, I found it comical and accepted the situation, quickly deciding to acquire new and adequate selling tools.

I began by setting up meetings with all the dealers listed in my books during the first week. The purpose was to introduce myself, understand their businesses, and strategize on how we could kickstart this program. My very first meeting was with two brothers who owned a janitorial supply company in Queens. As I arrived at their facility, I could not help but notice the barbed wire on the windows and graffiti on the building's sides. To enter, I had to use the intercom and wait for them to buzz me in. In that moment, I started questioning what I had gotten myself into.

Inside, I was greeted by an elderly receptionist to whom I mentioned my appointment with Ernie. To my surprise, she turned her head and yelled, "Ernie, your appointment is here!" Unfortunately, there was no response from Ernie. Eventually, he appeared at the front and scolded the woman, saying, "Hey, what the hell did I tell you about not interrupting me and yelling when we have a guest?" His stern and belligerent tone caught me off guard. He then looked at me and said, "So, you must be the new Windsor guy. I'll give you five minutes before I kick your ass out of here."

Refusing to back down, I firmly held onto his hand and replied, "Ernie, you don't know me, and I don't know you. But one thing's for sure: you'd rather have me selling on your team than selling against you." I looked him directly in the eyes as I spoke. Surprisingly, he reciprocated the intensity and said, "My man, somebody with a lot of balls. I love it. Come on back, and let's see what we can do together."

In that moment, I realized that as a salesperson with nothing to lose, it is essential to take risks, be bold, and exude confidence.

From that day forward, I established a wonderful relationship with Ernie and his team, and together, we achieved remarkable success in selling equipment. Once you overcome the initial hurdle of convincing the owner, the next challenge is to win over the DSRs (distributor sales representatives) and prove that you are worth their time. The key is to understand what motivates each individual and capitalize on it, as everyone has different interests. By helping them make money, you will ultimately make money yourself. However, it is crucial to prioritize this order, or you will never reach the pinnacle of your selling career. Interestingly, I later discovered that the wonderful woman at the reception desk was Ernie's mother. Family businesses often possess a variety of personalities, and that may just be the secret to their success.

New Yorkers often receive a bad reputation for their aggressive nature, but consider me biased, I found it to be quite the opposite. It was the "can-do" attitude that made a successful salesperson. Countless times, I heard phrases like "let's go" and "let's go make a decision." I referred to New York as an up-tempo city, always seizing every opportunity. The adage that if you can sell in New York, you can sell anywhere holds true.

I embarked on my first rep/customer call in February '88 with Willie, a salesman working for Ernie, who took me to a property management company to demonstrate our vacuums and our industry-first self-contained extractor. One thing I was confident in was my ability to impress customers with the equipment I represented. I religiously practiced the new techniques I learned and applied them to show the value to the audience, essentially how it would make their jobs easier. I would even go to a local school to rehearse and audition myself doing demonstrations. Back then, I remembered Charlie saying that the sale was made at the point of demonstration, and it was true.

During the demonstration, I wowed the customer, and he turned to Willie and asked for the price. To my dismay, Willie priced the product at 15 percent over the suggested manufacturer resale price. The customer immediately responded, saying, "You can do better on price." Willie's pitch was that Ernie would be furious, but he would give the customer a whopping 15 percent discount. However, he emphasized that he would be in deep trouble. The customer, seeing the pain on Willie's face, agreed, and said, "Okay, give me two of the extractors and a dozen vacuums." In my mind, I quickly calculated that I would earn a little over $1,000 in commission. Since we only had about a dozen products in our line, it was easy for me to calculate commissions for every sale.

As we left, I turned to Willie and asked if inflating the MSRP (manufacturer's suggested retail price) was a customary practice for him. He looked at me and said, "I do it on every call. Everyone likes a discount. I will not sacrifice my commissions. Start high, bring it down, and make your margin." I looked at him and jokingly said, "So, you never want me to show our MSRP price schedule?" We laughed, and he replied, "I'd have to shoot you if you did."

Just up the block was one of my premier distributors, a family, a father and two sons' combination. They had a substantial number of property management companies in their customer portfolio. To earn their trust and respect, I went out with the brothers to do some demos, and they quickly realized that I could help them make money. They jokingly said among the three of them, "we need to hire this guy, we are batting 1,000." This marked the beginning of a wonderful relationship.

Here's a sight for all professional salespeople calling on the streets of metropolitan markets. One day, I remember picking up Barry, one of the sons, at his warehouse, and to my surprise, an elderly gentleman who reminded me of Mickey, the trainer for Rocky in the movie, jumped into my van, he was Johnny, our driver. Since my van only had two seats, Johnny had to sit in the middle on an upside down, five-gallon bucket. I later learned that this was a frequent practice in the city due to the inflated cost of parking, which was $11.00 per hour. With a van full of equipment, we would go to do the demo, and if the police showed up to move the van, Johnny would drive around the block a few times until we finished and were ready to load up for the next demo.

During that time, I had certain rules of engagement. If someone booked me for a full day, I expected a minimum of four qualified demos. Anything less would be a waste of my time. Since we did not have cell phones back then, I had to pull over and use pay phones for communication. I always made sure I had plenty of change for these inconvenient devices, which were quite challenging to find in the city! You could imagine how grateful I was for the invention of the car phone.

The biggest sale of my career happened within just two hours, with Barry and our driver, Johnny. As I picked them up, Barry looked at me and said, "You better have your *A* game today. I'm getting you in front of the main guy who operates sixty large high-rises in Manhattan." I turned to him and asked, "Did you bring your order pad?" Excitement filled the air as we arrived at the building and met Tom, the property manager. He showed us the dirtiest area, which was perfect for our demonstration. Sensing his time was valuable, I politely asked for a few minutes to set up. Tom agreed and thanked us, promising to check back in ten minutes. Taking the time to set up is key, as it ensures everything is in working condition and that there are electrical outlets nearby. I prepared the extractor by adding water and chemicals, and with just one pass, the carpet looked brand new. Another important aspect is not shying away from their worst area and biggest pain point. I had brought my vacuums along, despite Barry's suggestion not to show them. I insisted, knowing that Tom would also be interested in purchasing them. When Tom returned, I pointed to the vacuum and displayed its impressive features. To my delight, he expressed his frustration with cheap vacuums that kept breaking down and showed a keen interest in the uprights I presented. Moving on to the extractor, I made a single pass in the middle of the hallway and was amazed at the transformation it achieved on the carpet. As I began rolling up the cable, Tom could not believe I would leave his carpet in that state, so I squared it off. He turned to Barry and instructed him to take notes, as he went on a rampage, ordering extractors and vacuums for at least sixty buildings. That one demonstration resulted in my commission count of approximately $32,000. Not bad for a morning's work!

As we left the building, Barry turned to me and exclaimed, "It's time to party!" It was only 10:00 a.m. in the morning, but we hopped into the van with Johnny at the wheel and headed to Forty-second Street to celebrate eat, drink, and enjoy the company of dancers. We spent a delightful three hours having a blast, but more importantly, bonding over the teamwork. I glanced over at Johnny, who had a wide smile on his face, and remarked, "Boys, I could get used to this. When is the next big sale expected?" I replied, "Barry has to get off his ass and get us more opportunities." Later, as I dropped off the guys at the warehouse, I pulled Barry aside and asked how we should take care of Johnny. Barry assured me not to worry, as he had it covered and would get him a couple of bottles of wine.

That night, as I made my way back to the Red Roof Inn, I could not help but exclaim, "God, I love this job!" It was just the beginning of remarkable things to come. I remember arriving late in the evenings and waking up early in the mornings, unable to contain my excitement for what the next day would bring. I portrayed a sense of confidence that was infectious. I knew my products and the inner workings to the nut and bolt. I also studied competitors' products so I could point out their weaknesses as well as give them credit where credit was due.

I also worked closely with another distributor that had two partners and some sons involved in the business. They became great customers of mine. I call to mind one day when Bobby was incredibly excited because he had secured a demonstration at Yankee Stadium. Our task was to clean George Steinbrenner's office, the owner of the Yankees. After passing through security, we met the facilities manager and made our way up to the office. The carpet in the office had coffee spills and grease stains. The facilities manager expressed his desire to be able to clean the carpet themselves, as they believed contractors never did an adequate job. The carpet was navy with a large white NY logo. Unfortunately, we made one fatal mistake—we did not ask if the carpet was made of wool.

Despite this oversight, the demonstration went exceptionally well, and the carpet looked brand new. We thought we had sealed the deal. However, the next day, Bobby called me in a frantic state. He explained that Steinbrenner was still out West but would be returning soon, and they had called him upset about brown streaks running through the logo on the carpet. I chuckled and reassured Bobby that it was not a major concern. It must have been wool carpet, and all they needed to do was use a product called brown out to rinse the carpet. They followed my advice, used the brown out, and reported that the carpet looked great. As a result, they were ready to purchase many machines.

One memorable night, I had the opportunity to work with Bobby's father, Jules, down on Wall Street. I met Jules at his office at 10:00 p.m., and we headed into Manhattan. We arrived at the first building around 11:00 p.m. that night, where Jules had gathered the entire crew. We proceeded to demonstrate the vacuums and extractors, and they were a hit. The crew loved them and started discussing how many they needed. We moved on to the next building at 2:00 a.m. in the morning and repeated the process. By sunrise, we had sold a significant amount of equipment. We sat at a diner overlooking Hudson Bay, enjoying breakfast, and laughing about what a fantastic evening we'd had. Jules looked at me and remarked, "My friend, we are the last of the Mohicans." He went on to express doubt that anyone else was out there doing what we had just done, as most people were at home sleeping. He concluded by saying what a pleasure it was to collaborate with me and called me a true professional. Jules was exemplary, and his company quickly became one of my top three customers. This experience taught me that the time and effort you put forth will align with your financial goals. I also took to heart Jules' comment about making money while others sleep and frequently use that line.

Word was spreading about this young, aggressive guy from Windsor. The Advance rep and the Clark rep were both threatened by the potential loss of their loyal distribution for carpet equipment.

One of the more amusing stories involved a distributor on Long Island. This distributor, a staunch supporter of Advance, was planning a carpet seminar and invited Gordy, an industry expert on carpets, to present. I found myself pitted against Advance. I spoke to Gordy and expressed my belief that it was unfair for him to position my products against Advance's, as their products were clearly inferior. Gordy shared dislike for Advance and promised to lead them down the path of failure. During the seminar, we started with the vacuums side-by-side, and it was evident to the audience that ours was superior. The comedic moment came during the demonstration of the self-contained extractor. The Advance Tempest failed to pick up the water, so after the Advance Rep, Jim, finished his demonstration, I announced to the audience that I would go back over his area with a clean recovery tank to show how much water he had left in the carpet. I poured the water into a white five gallon bucket, astonishing the attendees with the amount I pulled out. I then did a side-by-side comparison, which wowed the audience. Jim approached me and accused me of putting Gordy up to it. I simply replied, "Jim, there's a new kid on the block. I look forward to competing against you." As you will see later in the book, Jim and I became close friends, and he eventually took my spot as the Windsor rep, doing an outstanding job of growing the market.

Another seminar I remember took place in Queens. I did not have much time to find a soiled carpet for the demonstration, so on my way up, I stopped in Atlantic City and searched trash dumpsters for any remnants of carpet. I found a heavily soiled white carpet, which looked like it had blood stains on it, resembling a crime scene. When I arrived at the seminar, Paul asked me where I found the carpet, and I replied, "In the dumpster in Atlantic City." We laughed together as we examined the carpet. Paul suggested we go heavy on the pre-spray to demonstrate the extractor's ability to remove the stains in one pass. As Paul presented the equipment to the attendees, I continued spraying the pre-spray. Unfortunately, the pre-spray became airborne due to the fans and filled the room with its odor. One attendee jumped up and exclaimed, "What are you trying to kill us?" Paul turned to me and suggested we put the pre-spray away for now. Despite this mishap, the seminar was successful, and we sold a significant amount of equipment. Afterwards, we laughed about the incident and the gentleman who accused us of trying to harm him, jokingly said afterwards, "Great job guys, I'll send you my medical bills."

The Importance of Time Management

I was determined to be more efficient and took the initiative to research car phones, which were just emerging in the market at that time. Fed up with constantly searching for pay phones, I decided to invest in a car phone, despite its bulky size resembling a small duffel bag. However, my first mistake was distributing my number to everyone I knew. Nevertheless, I utilized the phone to receive calls and arrange demos, ensuring I stayed in front of customers to make sales.

Unfortunately, Brenda received the bill for the first month, which amounted to over $800. Despite the hefty expense, I never regretted the investment due to the money it helped me generate. One amusing anecdote that often came up during bar conversations involved a situation with a DSR. While traveling uptown on Fifth Avenue after two morning demonstrations, I asked him if he had any demos lined up for the afternoon. When he replied negatively, I quickly made a few calls and managed to arrange demonstrations in White Plains. I pulled over to the side of the street and informed him that he needed to get out. Startled, he questioned if I was just going to leave him there. I responded affirmatively, feeling guilty and giving him $20 to catch the subway or train. I had to prioritize making money and could not afford to waste an entire afternoon. This incident became a topic of discussion among industry professionals for many years.

To expand my business on Long Island, I knew I had to take on another distributor and find innovative ways to promote my brand in the marketplace. So, I produced a creative solution by partnering with a distributor that the larger distributor disliked. I began collaborating with her to sell a variety of products on the island, which caught the attention of the bigger distributors. I can recall nights after 8:00 p.m., knocking on Marian and Jules' door, urging them to join me for late-night demonstrations. I would tell them to get on the phones and call their customers, emphasizing the importance of our work. Initially, they thought I was ridiculous, but it worked. They knew I was dedicated to growing their business, so that night, Marian contacted a manager at the Old Westbury Country Club, where the owner of the big distributor was a prominent member. Marian successfully conducted the demo and secured an order. I received a call from the owner, expressing his disbelief that I had sold machines to his country club. I confidently confirmed the sale and mentioned that it could have been his if he did not prioritize loyalty to Advance. This incident opened doors for me, and my business on Long Island began to flourish rapidly.

As I pursued my goal of reaching $180,000 in commissions, I attended the international restaurant show at the Javits Center with my colleague, Paul. We had an incredible time at the show, realizing that our equipment was in high demand within the hospitality industry. During the event, we even took a bold approach by grabbing people's plates as they passed by the chicken wings booth. We would throw the wings on the floor and demonstrate how our equipment efficiently cleaned up the mess, leaving people astonished. This daring tactic resulted in numerous leads, helping me run up my commissions. It just goes to show that if you are at a trade show and aiming to make sales, you need to be creative in your approach. Do not hesitate to engage with people, pull them into your booth, and have meaningful conversations. You will be amazed at the positive outcomes that come from working hard and actively promoting your products or services at these events.

Designing a National Account Program

After gaining some familiarity with the New York metropolitan market, I unexpectedly received a call from Charlie and Tom. Tom, the owner of Windsor, expressed his gratitude during our conference call for my swift turnaround of the Metropolitan New York territory. Both Charlie and Tom believed that I should expand my role to a national level. They offered me the position of national account manager, which would involve a financial setback but also presented an opportunity for personal growth within the company. This would be a step back in terms of finances, but a leap forward in terms of career advancement. They expressed their interest in hearing my ideas for a national account program and invited me to fly out to Englewood, Colorado to discuss my thoughts on a forward-thinking program.

I arrived in Denver in the spring of 1989. During our meeting at the plant, I witnessed firsthand the "can-do" culture. I presented my vision for what would later become the Prime Account Program. Drawing from my experience in the wholesale distribution industry, I emphasized the importance of setting ourselves apart from our competitors, Advance and Clarke. These competitors offered national accounts a standard 40 percent discount off MSRP, but they lacked a comprehensive program that truly benefited multi-location corporate accounts. Their focus was solely on price, which left a gap in meeting the needs of these accounts. To address this, I proposed a simple yet effective differentiation strategy: renaming our program as the Prime Account Program. This shift in name association would signal to distributors that they were not excluded from the equation, but rather integral to the program's success. Instead of receiving only a small incentive for setting up equipment, distributors would now have a more significant role and be recognized as prime partners in our program.

The Prime Account Program implemented a pricing structure that offered a 15 percent discount off MSRP. This pricing strategy ensured a 25 percent profit for distribution participation, providing a strong incentive for distributors to actively engage in the program. With Windsor's successful development of key distribution channels nationwide, it was important to further accelerate growth by aggressively targeting corporate accounts and driving profits throughout our distributor network. To streamline operations and maintain consistency, we introduced the Prime Account price book, which served as a standardized reference for all sales. Additional discounts were eliminated, and our focus shifted towards highlighting the comprehensive benefits of the program. One of the primary differentiators we incorporated was the inclusion of freight costs, simplifying the process for corporate accounts. To reinforce our branding identity and communicate important instructions, we designed large labels that were placed over the opening flap of each box. These labels explicitly informed corporate accounts not to open the box until authorized training had been established.

The preferred distributor in each market was promptly notified through the Prime Account system whenever a shipment was scheduled for their area. This notification included all relevant information about the local corporate accounts, enabling the distributor to proactively reach out and arrange for equipment uncrating and personnel training. To ensure accountability and proper documentation, we introduced a postage-paid return card that was attached to the warning label. Both the distributor's installer and the receiving corporate account manager were required to sign this card and send it back to our Prime Account department for processing. Upon receipt of the signed card, the distributor would receive a 25 percent credit. In cases where we did not receive a card authorizing the installation and training, the corresponding funds were allocated to a separate account known as the Prime Account kitty.

We positioned the program as offering superior and innovative products that effectively reduced labor costs. Additionally, we emphasized the added value of providing free freight, professional installation, and comprehensive training. To further enhance customer satisfaction, we ensured that each corporate account had access to local support through their designated distributor service center. This not only facilitated immediate service assistance but also created opportunities for the distributor to upsell ancillary items to the account. By opening doors of opportunity, we recognized that sales are about mutually beneficial partnerships. Through a cooperative effort, we aimed to maximize earnings by helping one another succeed.

I established my office in Ocean City, New Jersey shortly after my return from Denver. I enlisted the assistance of a secretarial pool to oversee administrative and clerical tasks. However, I recognized the importance of remaining actively engaged in pursuing potential business opportunities and working alongside our territory managers in the field. Extensive research was conducted to develop a robust pipeline of prospects. To maximize efficiency, I classified and prioritized these opportunities, ensuring that my schedule was filled with productive meetings. I had devised a successful system for prospecting, which involved making calls on Fridays to schedule meetings for travel two weeks in advance. Through experience, I discovered that late morning to early afternoon on Fridays was the optimal time for cold calling or prospecting. Prospects were in a positive mindset, looking forward to the weekend, and more receptive to discussing opportunities and confirming business meetings.

Over the course of the following year, I dedicated forty-four out of fifty-two weeks to being on the road, consistently leaving on Sundays and returning on Thursdays, with Fridays reserved for making calls. This repetitive schedule allowed me to maintain a consistent presence and drive the success of the program. The program's structure, which rewarded distribution and provided full commissions to our territory managers, further solidified its potential for success. Prior to my arrival in each town, I would notify our territory manager, who would have all the necessary equipment loaded in their vans. Together, we attended prequalified headquarters meetings, where I specifically highlighted and sold the program, rather than just the individual products. By demonstrating our unique and innovative products, we generated excitement and enthusiasm among potential clients.

I remember a meeting with a prominent hotel chain; one of the largest in the world, where we demonstrated our upright vacuums. Initially, they expressed skepticism about investing three times the amount on an upright vacuum. However, we took the opportunity to highlight the numerous benefits of our machine, which sparked their curiosity. Despite this, they remained dissatisfied with the pricing. In response, we proposed a solution: the only way for them to completely understand the value of our product was to give it a chance and evaluate its benefits over an extended period. We suggested a four-month guaranteed trial order (referred to as a GTO). To our surprise, they agreed. During the trial period, they were pleasantly surprised by the durability of our machine. They noted that the units they had previously purchased required frequent maintenance and replacement, whereas our vacuum held up exceptionally well. Additionally, they involved their marketing department in highlighting the benefits of improved indoor air quality, which contributed to enhanced customer satisfaction. The evaluation proved to be a resounding success, with measurable results and clear savings that solidified the value of our product. Our territory manager, Bob, demonstrated exceptional skills in managing the account. We experienced significant success with a large Prime Account, which not only purchased our upright vacuums but also expanded their order to include our complete carpet cleaning systems. We effectively sold them the bundle, showcasing the benefits of the entire system.

Another notable opportunity arose when we engaged a national rental company, in search of a small self-contained extractor. During our meeting with their senior engineer and senior project manager, we highlighted the advantages of our machine. I distinctly remember the project manager turning to us and asking for the price if they were to purchase four thousand units. "I explained that the price would depend on our company's ability to negotiate reduced costs for volume, purchased components from suppliers, which we would then pass on to them." It is worth noting that I did not discount the price outright. Instead, we focused on identifying savings without compromising our margin. As a result, they proceeded to purchase thousands of units and became strong advocates for our brand.

The service contracting business experienced rapid growth, and we actively pursued partnerships with top-rated national companies. Among the numerous request for proposals (RFPs), one particularly stood out as the significant opportunity that slipped away. We were actively pursuing this large service provider based in Manhattan. I went above and beyond to fulfill all their requirements and even presented innovative ideas to enhance their business, without receiving anything in return. This experience taught me a valuable lesson: always secure a commitment before offering valuable ideas or resources. I believe that my presentation to their committee surpassed those of our competitors. However, it is important to acknowledge that failure is a part of the learning process. I realized that one should never assume they have secured a business deal until they are officially set up in the client's system and have a confirmed purchase order. Looking back, it was their loss, as our company subsequently made significant strides in the cleaning industry.

Tom popped into my office one day and said, "Do you see how much money has accrued in the Prime Account kitty?" While I acknowledged that I was aware it was significant, I admitted that I had not checked it recently. "It has surpassed $100,000, and for the life of me, I can't understand why our dealers are not capitalizing on the program," Tom said. I reassured Tom that if our distributors were not taking full advantage, we would have our territory managers in place who were receiving full commissions to manage installation and training. I assured him that the local touch with that corporate account was being nurtured and maintained.

One day, I received a call from the owner of a prominent regional distributor located out West. Charles called expressing his frustration over losing a sale due to another distributor offering a significantly lower price on a couple of extractors, resulting in a $2,500 loss in profit. Knowing that this distributor was a dedicated supporter of Windsor, I quickly asked if he had access to a nearby fax machine. He informed me that his secretary, located just outside his office, had one and provided me with the fax number. Apologizing for the interruption, I requested a brief hold and instructed my administrative assistant to deduct $2,500 from our kitty and credit it to this distributor. I emphasized the urgency, asking her to complete the transaction and fax the credit memo to the provided number within the next few minutes. Once I returned to the call with the owner, I engaged in a conversation about one of his expansions, allowing a few minutes to pass before inquiring if his fax machine was buzzing. He called out to his secretary, who promptly brought in the credit memo for $2,500. I will always remember his remark, expressing his appreciation for our company's commitment to standing by our actions, regardless of the consequences. We strategically utilize the kitty to create a "wow" factor when working with our distributor network.

During that time, we experienced significant success in securing hotel business. Our product offerings were primarily focused on carpet care, and given the prevalence of carpets in those days, this proved to be a lucrative market. We were fortunate to have unique and innovative products that effectively addressed common problems, simplified tasks, and had a comprehensive support program in place. This ensured that our machines were used correctly and remained operational. We understood the excessive cost of downtime, especially without access to local service and support.

The Prime Account program was designed to be distributor friendly. It is worth noting that our two major competitors, Clarke and Advance, offered comprehensive product lines for both hard surfaces and carpets. To incentivize distributors to shift their purchases to our brand in these categories, our program provided attractive benefits. We genuinely cared about the success of our distributors' businesses, their profit margins, and their return on investment. This approach played a significant role in propelling our brand to become a leader in the industry.

Creating a sales program that sets you apart from competitors and clearly defines the benefits and measurable outcomes for all parties involved is crucial. The success of the Prime Account program can be attributed to our ability to precisely achieve that. It is evident that price alone is not the determining factor; instead, it is about selling a program that delivers measurable results and long-term advantages for the customer.

The program gained significant momentum over the course of the next twelve months, reaching several million dollars in revenue. I remember receiving a call from Charlie on Thanksgiving Day, informing me that he and Tom were discussing my next role within the company as the national sales manager. However, they mentioned that I would need to relocate to Denver, with a target start date of January 1. This left me with limited time to gather my thoughts and plan, especially considering the impact on my family. After careful consideration, I packed my bags on December 31 and made the move to Denver. I ensured that the Prime Account manager position was filled by a highly capable individual named Joe, who excelled in the role. Joe went on to hire additional Prime Account managers, each focusing on specific business classifications, and they did an outstanding job of taking the reins. Initially, I expected to stay in a temporary apartment for a brief period, but due to the challenging housing market, it ended up being a duration of eighteen months. It was a challenging time as I only had the opportunity to visit my family once a month.

Sales Management

I had the privilege of working with Paul, the vice president of sales, in my role as the national sales manager. I held a great deal of admiration for Paul due to his professional approach to business. Together, we collaborated on developing and implementing strategies to enhance distribution sales for the company.

Our distribution philosophy was straightforward: to establish a solid foundation that would enable distributors to profit from selling building maintenance equipment. We aimed to provide a better return on investment compared to our competitors. Our mission was to secure the top distributor in each market and actively promote our brand. We achieved this by offering exclusive or semi-exclusive partnerships, which played a significant role in our success. The brand experienced tremendous growth in the market due to our unwavering commitment to our distributors. We prioritized training and continuously educated our partners on our products, even inviting them to our plant on many occasions. Additionally, we tried to understand our customers. It is highly recommended to go beyond their business and get to know them as individuals. By investing in building relationships, you will be pleasantly surprised by the personal benefits that arise from this effort.

We were fortunate to have an exceptional marketing manager named Carv. I vividly remember a day when he was collaborating with Charlie on creating a tagline for the upcoming industry trade show. He proposed the tagline "The Distributor Is King," and it perfectly aligned with our business philosophy. We designed all our sales programs with the goal of maximizing the profitability of our distributors and their sales teams. Our core principles revolved around consistently doing what was right for our customers in every situation.

One of our primary business objectives was to align ourselves with the top performers in the industry, which is where the Triple-S Association played a crucial role. As mentioned in earlier chapters, this association consisted of the most exceptional distributors in the country. Through negotiations, we secured a private brand for several products, which granted us access to this esteemed group of distributors. Our strategy of collaborating with this association proved to be successful, as it allowed us to expand our reach and gain valuable coverage. Personally, I found great satisfaction in developing enduring relationships with the Triple-S management team and their members across the country. As you will discover later in the book, this investment paid off significantly for me.

There was another association that greatly contributed to the growth of our equipment line. This association was known as IEHA, which stands for the International Executive Housekeeping Association. I recall picking up Beth, their CEO, from the Denver airport. During our drive to meet the executive team and present our NBA (national brand alliance) pitch, we discussed the significant participation fee. I expressed my belief in her program and how it would benefit our company, especially since much of the membership was in the healthcare industry. Our products were a perfect fit for their needs. During the meeting, Tom, our owner, listened attentively and then asked about the return on this substantial investment. We assured him that the exposure alone would prove worthwhile within a year. Tom turned to Beth and confidently said, "Where do I sign?" Joining the NBA was the right decision, as it led to substantial growth in our healthcare segment. IEHA, like Triple-S, has been my closest ally and confidante throughout my career.

During my tenure as the national sales manager, I had the privilege of crossing paths with a remarkable individual named Harvey, who served as the president of a prominent paper company in Texas. Harvey stood out due to his unwavering passion for the industry and his firm grasp on what was necessary for his company's success. There were two instances in my early career where I gleaned invaluable insights from him. His company provided unwavering support to us in the state of Texas. At one point, we were considering a change that had the potential to derail our progress and prove immensely challenging to recover from. As we sought avenues for growth, we engaged in discussions with various national wholesale companies. One such prospect was Grainger, and negotiations had been ongoing for some time. Their fervent desire to partner with us stemmed from the widespread acceptance of our brand. After meeting with the corporate management team at Grainger, we collectively concluded that it had the potential to be a suitable partnership, provided we effectively managed any conflicts that might arise in the market.

Paul and I were entrusted with the challenging responsibility of informing our distributors that they would soon have a new competitor in their marketplace-Grainger. Paul personally traveled to the western region to meet with key distributors and deliver the news, while I boarded a plane to handle the distribution in the central and eastern states, ensuring they understood our position. I distinctly remember arranging a meeting with Harvey and entering his office. We engaged in a casual conversation about business before I proceeded to inform him of our intentions to establish Grainger on a national scale. Harvey astutely acknowledged that every action has a reaction, but he expressed utmost confidence that any issues that might arise would be swiftly and satisfactorily addressed. Harvey expressed his confidence in our decision and assured me that if we had his back, he did not foresee any significant issues. He understood the rationale behind our expanded business model. Subsequent meetings with other key distributors yielded similar responses. While some expressed disappointment, they acknowledged that it was a business decision and understood that we would have to wait and see if there were any repercussions from the increased distribution.

After Paul and I returned from our meetings with the key distributors, Tom called an emergency meeting. During the meeting, Tom said that he had been inundated with phone calls from distributors and was now questioning whether our decision was the right move for the company. The management team collectively decided to reverse the decision and inform Grainger that we would not proceed with the partnership. Tom turned to Paul and me and instructed us to engage in damage control. We were tasked with revisiting the same distributors and reassuring them that we had reconsidered our initial decision. We needed to convey that we highly valued their business and acknowledged that sometimes companies make mistakes in assessing the potential ramifications of a decision. Fortunately, we had caught this error before it could cause any disruption in their respective markets.

I had arranged a meeting with Harvey, and upon arriving, I was greeted by his executive secretary who jokingly mentioned that he had been eagerly anticipating my visit all week. I sensed trouble as he had already heard the rumors of our decision reversal circulating in the industry. Word travels fast in our small industry. When I inquired about the meeting location, she informed me that Harvey had gathered his team in the boardroom. As I entered the room, I saw sixteen managers seated, waiting for me. I began to address the group, but Harvey interrupted and requested a moment to set the context for everyone present, ensuring a clear understanding of his perspective. I graciously yielded the floor to Harvey, although I must note that I had to tone down his rendition of the events. Harvey proceeded to express his disappointment, comparing our relationship to a marriage. He emphasized the trust he had placed in me as his partner and how he never expected me to betray that trust. In his eyes, we were inseparable, joined at the hip. "During this time, you were engrossed in conversations with a captivating entity named Grainger, and it seemed like a blossoming relationship. Unbeknownst to me, you were being unfaithful. Just as you were about to consummate this connection with the alluring Grainger, you abruptly changed your mind and said no, you could not go through with it. Now, I ask everyone in this room, can we trust him?" The room erupted in laughter, and Harvey turned to me, asking for my response. In that moment, I acknowledged that sometimes greed can cloud one's judgment. We had a moment of clarity and realized that if we could restore trust, our partnership would emerge stronger than ever. I learned that disrupting a successful program comes with consequences, risks, and the potential tarnishing of one's reputation.

Shortly after that, we introduced our revolutionary upright vacuum, which was a game-changer in the industry. I vividly remember a meeting with Harvey, Joe (his assistant), Paul, and Bill S., our manufacturer's representative in Texas. We presented the vacuum to them and suggested that an order for five hundred units would be appropriate. Harvey burst into laughter, and Joe jokingly asked if we had started drinking already. However, Harvey quickly changed his tune and recognized the potential opportunity. He instructed Joe to place an order for five hundred units and to hold us accountable for selling them. Filled with excitement, we left the meeting and headed straight to the bar. We celebrated our success with breakfast, lunch, dinner, before finally departing. The bill was quite hefty. We had an incredible time reveling in our victory. This experience taught us a valuable lesson-never underestimate the knowledge and eagerness of your customers to seize profitable opportunities. It was just the beginning of many more triumphs and enjoyable moments to come.

I had a scheduled trip to Edmonton with my Northwest sales representative, Marfield, to secure a partnership with a major distributor who had locations across western Canada. I asked Marfield how we could convince the owner, Reid, to commit to carrying our product line. Marfield suggested that Reid had a fondness for bourbon. So, we arranged a dinner meeting with him. We spent what seemed like hours drinking before we even started eating. Throughout the dinner, Reid continued to drink, and we knew it was time to kid around with him. I grabbed a napkin and began writing down the order. Reid insisted on seeing the napkin and exclaimed, "Let me see that damn thing, I may want to add more!" We assured him that it was time to make a commitment, and he signed the napkin. The next morning, we went to the office and informed the office staff that Reid wanted to proceed with the order for shipment. They attempted to contact Reid, but he must have had his phone turned off. They shook their heads in disbelief but proceeded to process the order and sent it to our company for further processing. We waited patiently, and around 10:45 a.m., Reid walked in, appearing as though he had a challenging morning. He sported sunglasses, and as he glanced in our direction, he raised them and jokingly said, "You didn't." We responded, "Oh, but we did! The ladies were ecstatic to process your order, and it's already being shipped." Laughter filled the room for several minutes, and Reid turned to us, remarking, "You guys are quite something." He then redirected our focus and requested our assistance in turning the inventory. From that point on, we forged a long-lasting and mutually beneficial business partnership that lasted for many prosperous years.

A similar incident occurred when my representative from Georgia and I had a scheduled meeting with our Atlanta distributor. Prior to the meeting, we had a conversation about how crucial it was for him to secure this order and regain good standing. Our meeting was with Ralph, the buyer, who had two distinctive traits. He suffered from an unfortunate disorder called narcolepsy, causing him to occasionally fall asleep during conversations. Secondly, he had a unique way of approving purchase orders; he used a self-inking rubber stamp. As we discussed the recommended purchase order, Ralph dozed off, providing us with an opportunity. We playfully adjusted his ink stamp. We changed it to the correct date and the next number in line for a purchase order. After a few minutes, he woke up and noticed the change, finding it amusing. I quickly apologized and informed him that we had also added an additional 10 percent discount to the order. Ralph laughed and exclaimed, "You guys are hilarious!"

The trade shows proved to be highly profitable for our company, delivering quick returns on our investments. We set up booths with dedicated representatives and provided them with clear instructions to secure as many orders as possible during and after show hours. We offered enticing specials to encourage distributors to bring their purchase orders to the show. One amusing moment stands out, involving a dealer from the Deep South. He entered our booth accompanied by his entourage, and the representative for that area asked if I could guide them through our product line and discuss the show specials. I agreed on the condition that they provide me with a list of the equipment they intended to purchase. Taking charge from the very beginning, I assumed the sale and let my New Yorker assertiveness shine through. As we swiftly moved through the booth, I demonstrated the benefits of each machine and confidently stated, "You'll need two of these, four of those, and three of these, etc." Eventually, I turned to our representative and requested to see the list. Based on the order they had compiled, I informed them that they would receive a 12 percent discount. Additionally, I will include a vacuum as a bonus. The owner turned to his buyer and asked, "What's the PO#? Do you have that purchase order?" We continued our conversation, sharing laughter and camaraderie. The owner expressed his gratitude, stating, "You sold me half of your booth and got us so excited that I didn't even realize how much I was spending." We thanked him for the order and mentioned that we looked forward to seeing him at our hospitality event later that evening.

We created an exceptional sales force, which we proudly considered the best in the industry. Charlie, our executive vice president, played a significant role in assembling this talented team and positioning our company for remarkable achievements within the industry. Our sales force reached the highest levels of success and garnered immense respect within the industry. We were fortunate to collaborate with outstanding distribution partners nationwide, and it was a pleasure working alongside their dedicated management teams, owners, and high-performing sales representatives in the field.

The camaraderie and culture that flourished within the company were truly exhilarating. We experienced rapid growth and had an abundance of fun along the way, leading our representatives to describe it as a once-in-a-lifetime journey. We not only made money but also genuinely enjoyed our work, creating a fulfilling livelihood. Our role as trusted advisors to distributors nationwide was highly valued, as they recognized the worth of our suggestions. As the saying goes, common success breeds further success, and this principle held true for us.

As all good things eventually ended, I made the decision to leave the organization to protect my representatives in the field. The catalyst for my departure was an executive change at the top, resulting in a new leader who previously oversaw our operations department. I vividly remember a lunch meeting at his country club, during which he posed a question that struck me deeply. He asked, "Do you think our salespeople are making too much money? I'm in favor of reducing their commissions." In that moment, I realized that I could never turn my back on the salespeople who had dedicated their blood, sweat, and tears to building this company. I responded firmly, stating that I was not in favor of commission reductions. He simply replied, "I'm sorry you feel that way." It became clear to me at that point that our future working relationship would not be a positive one.

One day, while sitting in my office, I received a call from a prominent regional powerhouse in the Midwest. The owner, Ames, was a successful businessman and one of our top distributors nationwide. During our conversation, Ames mentioned that he had made a change in his company's leadership and was seeking a replacement. As we delved deeper into the topic, he sensed my potential interest in the position and asked if I would consider it. I responded by telling him that my family and I were content in Denver, and I had no intentions of uprooting them. However, Ames persisted and reminded me that his company was not only one of our largest distributors but also a significant contributor to our success. He suggested that I at least come out to Indiana, to play a round of golf and discuss the opportunity further. Intrigued, I decided to hop on a plane and visit Indiana, which eventually became our home for the next twenty-six years.

Lessons Learned

- Create a thorough sales plan that includes a roadmap, timeline, and measurable goals.

- Find a mentor; Charlie was the best sales promoter in the industry.

- Be confident and assertive but avoid being arrogant and unpredictable.

- Don't lose sight of the bigger picture for the sake of minor gains.

- Take time to appreciate the present moment, cultivate meaningful business friendships, and try to stay connected.

- Remain steadfast in your beliefs and principles.

CHAPTER 4

THE MOVE TO THE MIDWEST

I was on my way to Indianapolis to meet with Ames and discuss a job opportunity at his company. He had a house located on the ninth hole of the golf course. I was ready to tee up for the first hole when Ames asked, "If you hit this one short in the fairway or hit it long in the rough, which ball would you hit next?" I answered, "Long and in the rough." He replied, "Risk taker, I like that." We decided to play the first nine holes before settling down on the ridge off his backyard to watch the golfers pass through. As we relaxed, we began discussing the industry, and Ames was curious to hear my thoughts on the future of distribution and the potential opportunities for regional companies like his. I mentioned that I believed the industry would eventually undergo consolidation, considering the current fragmentation with over four thousand distributors in the country. I expressed my support for Ames' regional occupation strategy and suggested that it could be expanded upon. Ames then shared with me his uncertainty about whether to position the company for sale, which he mentioned I could assist with, or to push forward and take it to the next level.

He sought my perspective on his company and what I believed was necessary to propel it to the next level. I responded by acknowledging the strengths of his company, such as its power lines–the strong reputable manufacturers HP Products represented, exclusivity, and healthy margins. I suggested that growth could be achieved through a combination of organic expansion and strategic geographic acquisitions. By pursuing this approach, he should be able to maintain his margins while simultaneously growing both through acquisitions and internal development. However, one challenge we identified was his aging sales force, and we discussed the importance of implementing an exit strategy for them to mentor younger salespeople and contribute to the company's future growth. This was crucial due to the loyalty and dedication of his senior representatives, who played a significant role in helping him attain a prestigious level. While considering the people aspect of the business, we also recognized the need for technological advancements and the importance of adapting, embracing change, and executing swiftly to keep ahead of the industry.

Ames was a flamboyant business leader; he brought every situation to life through his animated style. Ames suggested we make a quick stop at the warehouse to introduce me to some of the managers and take a tour of the facility. To my surprise, when we arrived, it was already 5:30 p.m., and his management team was gathered in the customer service area, surrounded by stacks of invoices. Curious, I asked Ames what they were doing, and he explained that they were reviewing each line item to ensure that the margins were aligned. If necessary, they would adjust accordingly. Later, I discovered that this was a customary practice among larger supply companies during that time. Instantly, I began brainstorming ways to protect margins and streamline the managers' workload, allowing them to go home at a reasonable hour. Speaking with them privately, I discovered that they had a great deal of respect for Ames and would stay until midnight if he requested it. Afterward, we went out for dinner and shared our visions for the future of the industry. Ames believed that I was the right person for the job and generously offered a compensation program. I mentioned to Ames that I needed to discuss the potential move with my wife and inform her about the possibility of relocating to Indianapolis, Indiana.

I remember that evening when I had a conversation with her and shared the news. She expressed some hesitation, remarking that Indiana was typically seen as a flyover state on our way back to Jersey. However, as you will discover later in the book, this decision turned out to be the best move we could have made for our family.

The following morning, Ames and I had breakfast, and I made the decision to accept the opportunity, fully aware that it would entail another transition for my family. It seemed ironic, or just bad luck, that the housing market in Denver was unfavorable. This situation mirrored my previous move out west, where I found myself living in an apartment for over year before my family could join me. During that time, I frequently traveled back and forth to Denver, making the most of the limited quality time I could spend with Brenda, Meaghann, and Connor. I made the difficult decision to prioritize my job to support my family, which unfortunately meant missing out on many important occasions that I can never get back. My daughter, Meaghann, even believed I was an airline pilot due to my frequent absences.

During my first week on the job, my focus was getting acquainted with everyone, understanding their roles and responsibilities, and familiarizing myself with company policies. I assessed the skill base and identified areas that needed improvement to achieve market dominance. The team had already experienced great success, but I believed a few adjustments were necessary to propel the company to the next level. I recognized the importance of visiting a few of our top customers to gain a firsthand understanding of their opinions and preferences regarding our company. I distinctly remember my first meeting with a major automotive parts manufacturer. After the initial introductions, the operations manager remarked, "So, you're the person who will bring about positive change." The initial greeting was awkward, but it captivated me. I knew that a challenge was on the table and change anticipated. I suggested that we begin by discussing what they disliked about our company, as a starting point for improvement. He presented me with an invoice from Monday of that week and asked me to look. I asked him what specifically I should be observing. He then handed me an invoice from Wednesday and asked if I noticed any differences. He explained that they ordered the same products three times a week. Then, he paused for a moment and handed me the invoice from Friday. The customer expressed his primary complaint about our company: the prices were raised without any prior notification, at the discretion of the company. He emphasized that this was the main issue that needed to be addressed, and he believed that other customers felt the same way. He made it clear that while they appreciated their sales representative and valued our company, they desired the trust that prices would remain consistent over a certain period. They had budgets to adhere to, which were measured by their corporation, and they understood that prices could increase, but they requested that notification be provided to assist with planning.

Following the customer calls, my first recommendation to Ames was to implement a sliding scale for commissions. The idea was to reward salespeople with high margins and penalize those with low margins. However, I proposed giving them a grace period to make the necessary adjustments on their own. This decision was primarily driven by the desire to shift responsibility and align with the behavioral characteristics of the sales team. I drafted the sliding scale for further discussion, and as we analyzed it together, Ames looked at me and expressed his understanding. He acknowledged that I had only been with the company for a brief period, but he also recognized that I was suggesting a change to a twenty-five-year-old business practice that he had adopted when he started the company. Ames came from a retail environment where price adjustments were common. He gazed at me intently and asked, "How confident are you about this scale?" Without hesitation, I replied, "100 percent." Ames then responded, "Here's the deal: if we experience even a tenth of a percent loss in margin over the next twelve months, I reserve the right to terminate your employment." I met his gaze and confidently agreed, saying, "You've got yourself a deal." It was fascinating to observe how swiftly prices adjusted to reach the next level and maximize earnings once we implemented the scale. This experience highlighted the effectiveness of behavioral policies in helping salespeople excel in their roles.

The next area I focused on was improving our technology infrastructure to enhance our ability to promptly respond to customers' needs in the field. During that time, the Internet and websites were just beginning to make an impact on the industry. Recognizing the importance of visibility and branding, we swiftly developed a website. To further optimize our operations,

I conducted a thorough analysis of our sales process through flowcharting. This exercise revealed potential efficiencies that could be gained by investing in technology. Consequently, I embarked on researching bundled packages for hardware and software. With over one hundred salespeople spread across the Midwest and three branch locations, I needed to obtain quotes for laptops, software, and establish communication with our data manager to establish a connective link to our ERP system.

During my tenure at the manufacturer, I underwent a shift in focus from merely pricing products to actively selling them. To achieve this, I dedicated myself to creating various spreadsheets that encompassed not only equipment but also the ancillary products commonly sold in our industry. These spreadsheets formed a valuable library of resources, designed to guide customers through the decision-making process while ensuring they made the best long-term choices. Each spreadsheet concluded with either a straightforward cost savings analysis or a more intricate return on investment calculation, providing customers with a clear understanding of the potential benefits.

I gathered the quotes and arranged a meeting with Ames and our CFO to discuss the necessary investment for the project's viability. When Ames asked about the total cost, I informed him that it was slightly over half a million dollars. He leaned back in his chair, exchanged a glance with our CFO, and remarked, "I think Fisher's been hitting the bottle too much." He expressed disbelief, stating that we would not be spending half a million dollars and suggested shelving the idea for future consideration. Looking at both, I proposed an alternative approach: moving forward without requiring a single penny of the company's money. Ames, intrigued, responded, "I can't wait to hear this pitch." I confidently explained that I would rally the support of our one hundred sales representatives to fully embrace this transformation.

By implementing this program, the sales team would not only experience increased sales and margins but also gain efficiencies. They would have the ability to place orders directly in front of the customers, check stock availability, and most importantly, demonstrate why our products offered the best long-term solution and investment. Ames expressed skepticism, stating that the sales force would resist investing in such a program. I proposed a simple solution: we could secure a long-term lease and have the sales team pay a monthly fee, which would be automatically deducted from their paychecks. I assured Ames that I was eager to present this program to the sales force and suggested that the upcoming national sales meeting would be the ideal forum. Ames agreed, saying he could not wait to see the presentation and anticipated the sales team's reaction. I confidently affirmed that I would sell this program and gain buy-in from everyone. In sales, taking risks and not being afraid to fail is essential.

During the national sales meeting, Ames glanced at me and remarked, "I wouldn't want to be sitting in your shoes right now." I met his gaze and confidently replied, "Just be patient, you'll see." As each manager presented their respective topics, I patiently waited for my turn, which was saved for last. Taking the stage, I addressed the group and asked, "Are you all ready to elevate your knowledge, experience, and selling abilities to the next level?" A resounding "yes" echoed through the room. I proceeded to display several spreadsheets that demonstrated how they could achieve sales without resorting to product discounts. I emphasized the importance of educating customers about the total cost of ownership. The room filled with more enthusiastic affirmations, and some even shouted, "Show us the money!" I then posed the question, "How would you like to have the ability to present orders directly to your customers, check stock availability, and justify product costs at higher margins?" As I looked around the room, I could sense the growing excitement. It felt as if I were a colonel in the army, rallying and motivating troops before heading into battle. With the energy in the air, I proceeded to outline the plan, the compensation structure, and the commitment required to move this project forward. Then, I turned to the sales team and posed a simple question, "Are you willing to invest today to reap greater financial rewards in the future?" I requested a show of hands from those ready to embark on this journey with me. To Ames' surprise, every hand in the room shot up. It was a pivotal moment, marking our path towards becoming the first distribution company in the sanitary maintenance industry to equip our sales force with technology tools that would enhance their knowledge and deliver exceptional customer experiences.

We proceeded to place orders for the necessary hardware and software. Our data manager, Tom, did an excellent job connecting the ERP system to facilitate seamless ordering. The next step involved initiating the training process for our entire sales staff. While it required some adjustment for our senior representatives, they all embraced the learning experience as a positive step towards enhancing their professional careers.

Mergers and Acquisitions in the '90s

Ames played a significant role in my professional development and became my second mentor in the industry. What made our collaboration even more valuable was his immediate involvement in acquisitions. Given my prior experience at Windsor, I had established relationships with numerous distributors in the Midwest. This made it easy for me to reach out to them and inquire about their future, including their potential interest in selling their companies. However, I decided to take a different approach. I embarked on creating a marketing brand image video that displayed our company and the compelling reasons why distributors should consider joining our regional network. I sent this video to over three hundred distributors and soon began receiving inquiries from those interested in learning more about our initiatives and whether their company would be a suitable fit. One company in western Kentucky, having received our video mailer, decided to join our company through acquisition.

During our acquisition endeavors, we encountered several amusing anecdotes. One such story involved a prominent legacy company based in Lexington, Kentucky, which had been a staunch supporter of our product line during my time at Windsor. The owner of this company was a genuine southern gentleman who prioritized the well-being of his employees more than anything else. When I reached out to schedule a meeting, he initially felt a bit apprehensive, having heard rumors about our company's size and aggressive approach. He was uncertain about our history with previous acquisitions and whether we retained the employees of the acquired companies. Despite his reservations, he agreed to meet with us and graciously extended an invitation. As Ames, our CFO, Jan, and I made our way to the meeting, I emphasized the importance of approaching Jack, the owner, with utmost care and consideration.

As we arrived at Jack's company, we were aware that discussing potential changes with his staff to expedite our return on investment was a sensitive topic. Jack warmly greeted us at the door and proceeded to give us a tour of his facility. We then sat down to delve into the details of the acquisition and discuss Ames' initial plans. However, Ames could not contain his enthusiasm and quickly went on a rampage, suggesting numerous changes. I sensed trouble brewing, but we managed to salvage the situation by enjoying a pleasant dinner, engaging in fruitful discussions, and surprisingly, fostering camaraderie. Despite the positive atmosphere, I could not help but notice Jack's distant behavior, which raised concerns that he might be apprehensive about how his employees would fare under our ownership. On our way back to Indianapolis, I turned to Ames and expressed my belief that he might have gone a bit overboard with the changes, particularly within the different departments.

I believed that our approach might have frightened Jack, and I was uncertain if he would still be interested in selling. I distinctly remember Ames stating that Jack would sell to the company offering the highest monetary value. However, I expressed my belief to Ames that Jack's priorities lay with his employees rather than solely focusing on money. Ames countered, stating that he believed it came down to financial considerations. This potential acquisition held immense significance for our company, given the extensive presence Jack's company had throughout Kentucky. Then I received a call from Jack, informing me that he had decided to sell his company to another organization whose business philosophy aligned more closely with his own. Although he did not provide many details, I understood that he was referring to his employees' well-being. Sharing this disappointing news, I discovered that we had lost the deal to a company that offered a million dollars less but guaranteed no changes to the employees. In fact, they even provided raises.

We successfully pursued another acquisition, this time targeting a company located in our own backyard. This company was of comparable size to the one in Kentucky and boasted an exceptional sales force. When I informed Ames of my intention to contact the owner, he warned me that I might not receive a favorable response as the owner harbored animosity towards him. Our companies had engaged in intense battles and confrontations in the past, leaving doubts about any positive sentiment towards him. However, I believed that acquiring this company would be highly beneficial and yield a quick return on investment.

Undeterred, I reached out to the owner and managed to convince him to meet me for breakfast. During our meeting, he made it clear that he held a strong dislike for our owner, questioning the purpose of our meeting. I acknowledged his sentiments but emphasized that our industry was rapidly evolving. As an absentee owner, I advised him that the optimal time to sell and secure a favorable price for his company was now. I emphasized to the owner that every day he waited to sell his company, its value diminished due to the rapidly changing industry landscape. Despite his initial reservations, our meeting remained cordial, and we concluded by agreeing to stay in touch. Upon returning to the office, I shared the details of the meeting with Ames. He reaffirmed his belief that the owner harbored animosity towards him and insisted that our efforts were futile. However, I remained optimistic, as I had gleaned some valuable insights during our breakfast meeting. Two weeks later, Ames called me with surprising news; the owner had reached out to him and expressed interest in discussing the sale of his company. David, the owner, subsequently visited our office, and we successfully negotiated a deal. The next challenge was integrating the newly acquired company and addressing the delicate matter of sales territories. We worked swiftly to ensure that everyone was satisfied with the adjusted territories and that the transition was smooth for all parties involved.

We had another amusing experience during an acquisition attempt with a smaller company in Dayton, Ohio. The owner, Jack, greeted us at the door, and we proceeded to discuss our respective company philosophies. We decided to continue our discussions over lunch. As we got into Ames's Mercedes, Jack took the front seat while I sat in the back. Jack glanced around and complimented the car, to which Ames proudly replied that it was the top model. Jack then asked Ames if he liked Mercedes, and Ames responded affirmatively. Curiosity piqued, Jack inquired about the number of Mercedes cars Ames owned. Ames casually mentioned that they had two at their Florida home and three in Indianapolis. Sitting in the back seat, I could not help but think that we might not be able to strike a deal with Jack. It seemed like he would demand a significant amount of money for his company. On our way back to Indianapolis, we could not contain our laughter. I jokingly told Ames that he should not disclose the number of Mercedes cars he owned to potential sellers. We speculated that Jack might have thought he had hit the jackpot.

During my time at HP Products, we successfully acquired four companies, in addition to achieving organic growth that doubled the size of our business within a span of four years.

Shifting Landscape

The industry was undergoing significant changes, leading to a sense of restlessness among distributors nationwide. Many family-run companies were grappling with the decision of whether to pass the torch to the next generation or to sell and cash out. What most people in our industry were unaware of was that our company was the pioneer in considering a roll-up strategy, aiming to consolidate companies across the country. Ames and I extensively discussed the concept of worldwide distribution and sought the assistance of the law firm that had overseen the successful Sysco roll-up of independent food service companies. Leveraging my relationships with premier distributors throughout the country, I invited them to a meeting to discuss the formation of Worldwide. Approximately twenty-two distributed owners attended the presentation, and it became evident that joining forces would bring numerous benefits. It was akin to throwing your keys on the table, but the potential return was well worth it. The plan was to continue acquiring companies using their initial investments and eventually take the company public. However, there was one major obstacle in our path-the egos of the twenty-two individuals involved. The question of who would lead the company became a point of contention. Ames, who was spearheading the initiative, believed it was only fitting for him to assume the leadership role. However, others had differing opinions on how the organizational structure should be defined. Therefore, while the concept of Worldwide was promising from a conceptual standpoint, the execution fell short due to these internal disagreements.

I have vivid memories of traveling to Florida to visit Ames at his residence. Our trips consisted of both business meetings and enjoyable rounds of golf. During one of these visits, I noticed a familiar face just a couple of houses down; it was Greg Norman, the professional golfer. This sighting triggered a flashback to a Saturday meeting I had had with Ben when I first entered this industry. He had mentioned that selling toilet paper could be a lucrative endeavor. It is fascinating how life brings us full circle, reconnecting us with experiences that have shaped our professional careers.

We experienced steady organic growth through our power lines and exclusive agreements with suppliers. However, we began to encounter strain in these relationships due to unfortunate overlaps in our exterior branches, which created competition on our home front. Suppliers started demanding more from us. Here is a valuable tip: when you have a strong working relationship with suppliers, it is important to find ways to support and foster growth rather than taking a lackadaisical approach that might lead to conflicts in the market. Otherwise, the value of your product line diminishes in the eyes of distributor representatives. I distinctly remember a conversation with Ames where we discussed the need to establish closer ties with our suppliers. I suggested that we include a dedicated supplier section at our national sales meetings, where we could recognize and reward their support and achievements with us. This approach would help deter their expansion efforts with other distributors and strengthen our partnerships.

We made a deliberate decision to include the top suppliers and their representatives in our company meetings, and this initiative was met with great enthusiasm from all parties involved. The suppliers quickly became an integral part of our meetings, contributing their insights and expertise. We took the opportunity to recognize and appreciate their support by toasting the Supplier of the Year, Representative of the Year, and other notable awards. This gesture of recognition and appreciation proved to be highly beneficial for our business. We noticed that, as a result, we received more concessions and increased support from our suppliers, who were motivated by our acknowledgment of their efforts in helping us grow our business.

Creative Concepts

One of my career goals was to become a company president by the time I turned forty. At the age of thirty-eight, I had gained valuable experience in both wholesale distribution and manufacturing. I began contemplating whether it was time to move on and pursue further career growth. A situation arose that served as a catalyst for me to consider this direction. I shared my thoughts with Ames and the team, expressing the need to approach the university business from a unique perspective to secure 100 percent of their business. However, I also acknowledged the potential risk of losing the existing 35 percent of business if we proposed this change. This situation reminded me of a sales plan I had implemented earlier in my career at Ciba-Geigy, where we successfully alleviated pressure on the warehouse.

During our visit to the university, Jim, our representatives, and I engaged in a discussion about their expenses related to transporting products throughout the campus. We highlighted the costs associated with handling, maintaining vehicles, insurance, and infrastructure. We proposed an idea to them—what if they considered shutting down their storerooms to save a significant amount of money? The university officials liked the idea, but they informed us that, being a state-run institution, they would need to open the opportunity for bids. This meant that the business we had enjoyed could potentially be at risk if they decided to go with another company as the sole source. Despite this understanding, we remained optimistic and eagerly awaited the release of the request for proposal (RFP).

We convened a meeting with our management team to discuss our approach to the business and collectively agreed to establish a flat margin across the board. As I had an association meeting to attend, and Ames needed to return to Florida, we entrusted the management team with the responsibility of thoroughly reviewing the response before its submission. We emphasized the importance of careful examination to ensure that all aspects were considered and addressed appropriately.

I vividly remember receiving a call from the membership committee, who wanted to be the first to congratulate us on winning the RFP and the generous markup that we had granted them. I was taken aback and asked them to repeat what they had just said. They kindly obliged, and I specifically asked them to confirm if they were referring to the markup. They confirmed that indeed it was the markup they were referring to. I expressed our excitement as well and assured them that we were eagerly looking forward to the roll-out, execution, and planning phase. I emphasized the importance of mapping out clear and measurable expectations and objectives to ensure a successful partnership.

After receiving the award from the university, we were thrilled to learn that it would result in an additional $1.6 million in revenue. However, there was a snag in our response; we had mistakenly submitted a markup instead of a margin. When this error was brought to our attention, Ames became furious, realizing that we had potentially lost a significant amount of money. We needed to carefully consider how to address this situation. Later that day, we held another meeting, during which Ames informed us that he had his secretary draft a ninety-day cancellation letter. He asked me to go to the university and explain that we had made a clerical error. I expressed my concern, cautioning Ames about the potential consequences of this approach. I suggested that the committee might decide to award the business to the next company in line if they were dissatisfied with our response. Despite my reservations, Ames insisted that I make the necessary arrangements for the meeting with the university.

I met our representative, Jim, for breakfast at the university to discuss the situation. The diner was packed with students and Jim appeared to be nervous, not wanting to order any food. I had to deliver the news about the cancellation letter, and he expressed concern about the potential damage it could cause to both his family and income. He asked if there was any other way to resolve the issue. I reassured him that I had been considering alternative operational methods that could potentially offer a solution. We decided to meet with the committee and hear their perspective. During the meeting, I presented some options regarding routing and mapping of our delivery system. The committee seemed receptive to these minor modifications and accepted the proposed changes.

Jim and I decided to grab a cup of coffee to discuss the situation. He expressed concern about how I would explain it to Ames. However, I shared my calculations regarding the operational modifications, which led me to believe that we could not only recover the difference but potentially even gain more. On my way back, I received multiple calls from Ames's secretary, urging me to provide an estimated time of arrival and informing me that Ames wanted to see me as soon as I returned. When I finally met with Ames, he immediately asked if I had submitted the cancellation letter. I calmly explained that I had not, as I had worked out a mutually beneficial option instead. Ames became visibly upset and questioned what had changed. He asked if I worked for him or if he worked for me. I assured him that I had thoroughly vetted the alternative solution and believed it would result in a better outcome. Frustrated with the situation, Ames handed over the responsibility to me, demanding that I show him the details of the new plan.

After three months had passed, we conducted our first review. I received reports from our processing department, which confirmed that the operational adjustments had indeed resulted in gains. The university was thrilled with the implementation of the program and the significant cost savings achieved by shutting down their warehouse stores. I recall Ames returning from Florida and casually mentioning that we would be going golfing the next day, reminding me not to be late. As I had the supporting data on my desk, he picked it up while I engaged in conversations with sales reps. Ames briefly glanced at the data, placed it back on the table, and simply said, "See you tomorrow and don't be late for golf." It was challenging to admit that I had underestimated his reaction.

A simple acknowledgment or word of encouragement would have gone a long way in that moment.

Investing in Your Salespeople

During my final six months at the company, I dedicated myself to facilitating the next level of transition for our sales team. I introduced a program called the College of Values, which aimed to educate our team members on the importance of placing a value on everything we do for our customers and monetizing that value. The goal was to demonstrate to our customers the amount of money we were investing in them to ensure they received the desired results and support. This approach led to significant cost savings for both. I trained our salespeople on how to shift the focus away from cost and instead emphasize the value we provided. To support this initiative, I compiled a comprehensive book that categorized diverse types of value and provided insights on how to effectively sell based on value rather than price. This educational format, complete with tests and diplomas, empowered many individuals within the organization to differentiate themselves in the field, improve our company's image, and achieve significant competitive advantage.

I reached a point where I believed my time at the company had to come to an end. Ames was taken aback by my decision to leave and become the president of a smaller manufacturing company. Initially, I had been brought in to run his company while he planned to slow down and semi-retire. However, I soon realized that owners often struggle to let go of what they have successfully built. This experience would later resonate with me when I embarked on my own Greenfield start-up as a business owner.

Lessons Learned

- In a short timeframe, I was fortunate to gain a second mentor, Ames, who was legend in distribution.
- Share your knowledge and experience with others, empowering them to reach their fullest potential.
- Always keep your eyes on the future, envision what you want to achieve, and take action to create.
- Make mistakes; everything is correctable.
- Embrace change, as it brings new opportunities and is an inevitable part of business.
- Make sure to give recognition and praise when it is deserved.

CHAPTER 5

DISRUPTION FOR THE CLEANING INDUSTRY

In the nineties, a study was conducted that raised concerns among wholesale distributors regarding the future of their industry. This study extensively analyzed trends, providing both information and predictions. As a result, wholesale distribution companies and manufacturers came to the realization that their immature industry was undergoing rapid changes. It became evident that embracing and investing in these trends would prove advantageous for companies. While some of the study's findings and predictions materialized later than expected, they have nonetheless caused significant disruptions within the industry.

The study presented a comprehensive report supported by extensive research. It revealed that the existing business model was fundamentally flawed, and the impending changes would have a profound impact on both distributors and manufacturers. The identified trends were predicted to intensify in the following years, highlighting the fact that the traditional relationships between manufacturers and distributors were no longer effective and would undergo significant economic-driven transformations. While existing competitors were easily identifiable, the emergence of new competitors further disrupted the market by offering equivalent products.

The problem lay in the fact that the channel could no longer tolerate redundancies. Wholesale distributors had been complacent, taking growth for granted and neglecting the task of building new business, which was a significant issue. Additionally, retaining existing business had become a challenge. The study emphasized that distributors' sales force could no longer simply function as caretakers for customers; they had to find innovative ways to add value and differentiate themselves from competitors. Merely servicing the market was no longer sufficient to maintain a competitive edge against emerging rivals. At this point in time, wholesale distribution was more reactive than proactive, necessitating a shift in dynamics to safeguard their market share.

The study focused on the commoditization of the cleaning industry, where the determining factor often became who could offer the lowest price. Unfortunately, a competitive and fair market was lacking, which was a common issue across various industries. If one was not fortunate enough to have better purchasing power, the alternative was to differentiate themselves based on value. Another concerning aspect was the aging workforce within the industry, which lacked a younger generation to actively pursue and evaluate new candidates, let alone implement a retention plan.

Fortunately, I have a close friend who runs a successful consulting business that has made noteworthy progress in addressing this issue. When unable to attract new talent, the only option left is to either continue competing on price or invest in retraining salespeople to enhance their selling skills.

One of the key findings from the survey was the changing nature of customers, who were rapidly gaining access to information and becoming more knowledgeable than their sales representatives. This necessitated adaptation on the part of distributors, as failure to do so rendered them inconsequential. Companies that prioritized customer-centric approaches had a clear advantage, although they were scarce. It was crucial for sales professionals to recognize evolving customer needs and proactively develop innovative, value-added programs and solutions to secure their business. Unfortunately, many salespeople in the cleaning industry were preoccupied with selling their company's offerings without considering the functioning of their customers, the preferences of their employees, and most importantly, their primary cost-reduction initiatives.

The study raised questions about whether salespeople were truly customer driven. Upon observing the trend, it became evident that many salespeople struggled with cold calling or prospecting, often perceiving it as a waste of time due to potential rejection. A recommended practice was to initially categorize prospects into different enterprise buckets, conduct thorough research to gain insights into their business operations, and then tailor a targeted approach.

I believe that the success rate of closing a sale is heavily dependent on the preparation done prior to the call. By building a compelling case and demonstrating that you have done your homework, your confidence level will increase, and you will come across as more knowledgeable. This approach not only shortens the sales cycle but also increases the likelihood of securing more wins.

The subsequent question in the survey focused on meeting or surpassing customer expectations, which was where the distinction between a good and a poor salesperson became apparent. The key was to assess whether you had genuinely assisted the customer with their specific needs and whether you had respected their time by meeting or exceeding their expectations.

In today's fast-paced world, customers value salespeople who can provide solutions to their problems rather than simply pitching products. The customer profile has significantly evolved, with numerous options available to them. A valuable tip for salespeople in the present era is to leverage social media, which was not available in the past when we relied on door-to-door visits to establish contacts and uncover opportunities. Technology has empowered customers with extensive knowledge about products, if not more than the salesperson themselves. To stay ahead, it is crucial to profile customers and build a compelling business case that addresses their specific needs. There are numerous avenues available today for both in-person and virtual meetings. With the Internet, everything is easily accessible. It is safe to assume that customers are as knowledgeable about your products and services as you are. It would be an interesting experiment to transport today's salesperson back to the eighties, where they would have to adapt to a world without cell phones, laptops, or electronic scheduling calendars, relying solely on notepads and daytimers. Such an experience might foster a greater appreciation for effective time management.

Understanding the importance of customer segmentation is crucial. It requires building a comprehensive plan, like a business case, to identify which segments your solutions can effectively serve and what measurable advantages you offer. It is essential to remember that you are not just selling a product; you are providing solutions that customers can measure and evaluate. I always ask myself if the outcome I am offering aligns with what the customer desires. I then demonstrate how they can achieve that outcome in a shorter time. For instance, when someone enters a building, they do not typically admire the polished floors and ponder how long it took to achieve that level of cleanliness. Instead, it is important to determine the acceptable outcomes for each segment and tailor your business case to help them achieve those outcomes more efficiently, tapping into their labor budget. Salespeople must conduct thorough research on potential clients to effectively align their offerings with the client's needs. In the past, I would visit their facility and proactively identify areas for improvement even before the initial meeting. I would come prepared with potential solutions and ask targeted questions. However, in today's world, it has become increasingly challenging to gain access to facilities and survey the landscape due to a range of factors.

The study highlighted the necessary changes for salespeople to thrive in an evolving environment. I have always believed in a principle that prioritizes profitability, where the customer's profitability takes precedence over personal gain. It is crucial to identify areas of cost reduction that the customer may have overlooked, as these bring tangible value to the table. Finding cost savings is often easier than expected; it simply requires knowing where to look. I often refer to my previous statements on the importance of research. If 90 percent of a customer's budget is allocated to labor and only 10 percent to products, it is puzzling why many salespeople invest a significant amount of time in the 10 percent category. By dedicating more time to understanding and addressing the 90 percent labor bucket, salespeople can provide genuine solutions that result in the product being pulled through the process and a higher rate of return. Salespeople often focus their energy on the product bucket due to their comfort level. They may feel that they lack the necessary knowledge to delve into the labor side. However, I believe that the industry does not invest enough time or resources in educating salespeople about the significance of labor. To differentiate oneself from the competition, it is crucial to grasp the concept of labor and understand how to apply principles of reduction. The key is to determine how to make the job faster and simpler for customers while also considering the impact on budgets. It is important to establish a mechanism for measurement and consistently reinforce the value provided to customers, as they may sometimes have short memories.

The study addressed a crucial aspect: the changing relationship between manufacturing and distribution, which would lead to an imbalance in future sales dynamics. In the past, manufacturers dedicated significant effort to support their distributors in the field, fostering a sense of secure affirmation. During the nineties, there were over four thousand distributors nationwide, with fewer manufacturers compared to today. Relationships were built on work ethic and trust. The study predicted inevitable massive consolidation, which would strain and erode trust between manufacturers and distributors. However, I held a distinct perspective on the forecasted disruption and the number of distributors that would remain in the marketplace. It is worth noting that while massive consolidation did occur, it took place fifteen-to-twenty years after the study was conducted. The study suggested that consolidation would occur at a faster pace, potentially jeopardizing the survival of the industry if it continued its current trajectory. Consolidation can be advantageous for investors, as many consolidators are owned by private equity firms with the goal of building mass and either going public or selling for profit. However, there is now an opportunity for independent distributors to experience a resurgence by adopting a different approach in the market. Instead of focusing solely on pricing products, these independent distributors can differentiate themselves by selling solutions. When street margins begin to decline, it becomes increasingly challenging to achieve a satisfactory return on investment, regardless of the company's size. It is important to remember that in the supply chain, it is the distributor who often sacrifices margin. This margin compression has led to reduced support from manufacturers, as they face their own challenges in maintaining profitability. Salespeople have become accustomed to focusing primarily on pricing products, which has strained relationships and created a winning environment for customers. If this remains the prevailing approach, it is likely to continue being a chaotic situation. Master wholesale distributors play a crucial role in the industry by supporting smaller, independent distributors. These smaller distributors can stay in business due to the carrying cost of inventory and serve as a secondary source for larger distributors who need to meet zero backorder requirements.

When examining manufacturing trends, it becomes apparent that many manufacturers are bypassing traditional distribution channels. The reason distribution allows this is because they focus on selling the brand rather than offering comprehensive solutions. They may be content with lower margins, but this impacts the salesperson more than the owner. It is intriguing to observe that this issue revolves around pricing products. The solution to rebuilding street margins is straightforward: align with a manufacturer that values the role of distribution, one that has not saturated the market with various channels of access. Establishing an old-fashioned partnership based on measurable metrics is key. Instead of defaulting on selling based on price, it is pivotal to step out of the race to zero and utterly understand what the customer desires. By building solid business cases that address their needs, salespeople can differentiate themselves and thrive in the market.

The rise of online ordering and the entry of companies from outside the industry, such as packaging, office, and safety companies, have created a quick opportunity in the market. This phenomenon can be attributed to supply chain management and the cost to serve. Consolidating orders to a specific location can significantly reduce the cost to serve. However, it is important for these companies to carefully consider the margins associated with this combination before venturing into the janitorial supplies sector. While there may be a perceived need to diversify and increase importance within customers, it seems that everyone wants to enter the janitorial supplies market simply because it appears easy, and everyone is competing on price. This mindset further drives down street margins to uncomfortable levels. One key aspect that often gets overlooked is that 90 percent of a customer's budget is allocated to labor. It is unlikely that a packaging sales representative would have knowledge about the time their customer spends on floor stripping, nor would they have the inclination to learn about it. It is essential to find innovative ways to reduce labor, prioritize the customer's best interests, and ensure customer retention. By doing so, you will not only be selling a product but also offering a comprehensive solution that delivers measurable results.

I remember the early days of my professional career when selling products and solutions was an enjoyable and fulfilling experience. The industry was not as mature back then, and the relationships between manufacturers and distributors were close-knit and well-defined. When I first entered this business, I was fortunate to learn from manufacturers who took the time to educate and teach effective selling strategies. However, in today's mature market, there seems to be a lot of finger-pointing regarding whose responsibility it is to provide product training. What utterly amazes me is the word "product" itself, which should be eliminated from the cleaning vocabulary. Instead, the focus should be on how to bundle services and create solutions that have a direct impact on labor. I fail to understand why there is not more emphasis on teaching salespeople how to sell value and position solutions, rather than solely focusing on pricing products.

In the early years of working in this industry, distributors played a crucial role by stocking products and investing in inventory to ensure quick customer response. Manufacturers appreciated this arrangement as it allowed them to have their products available at multiple locations across the country. However, the landscape has changed significantly today, while customer expectations for fast delivery remain the same. The question arises: who bears the cost of fast delivery in today's market? Manufacturers are now adopting a build-to-order approach, which can delay meeting customer requirements. Distributors, on the other hand, are reducing their stock levels and relying on manufacturers to provide quick turnarounds on products. In the study, one of the criteria for evaluating a manufacturer from a wholesale distributor's perspective was gross margin. I have spoken to numerous distributors who have dipped into their backend rebates to offset the erosion of margins. It is difficult to find satisfaction in the current situation where backend rebates have become a necessary part of the cost of doing business. Previously, backend rebates were seen as an additional bonus. To correct street margins, it is crucial to align with the right manufacturer. Manufacturers need to recognize that their product alone is no longer sufficient in the market; it is just one component of a larger solution. The sooner both manufacturers and distributors understand this shift, the more market share they will gain and enjoy.

One area where the study fell short was in not giving enough importance to volume buying incentives, commonly known as rebates, in their evaluation. In today's market, these incentives have become a top priority for distributors as they strive to combat street margin erosion. However, relying solely on back-end rebates to offset margin losses can be a precarious path to take. The real solution lies in correcting street margins themselves. There is no excuse for neglecting training in this area, especially with the technological tools available today that can swiftly demonstrate a distributor's value in an account. Information is a powerful tool that is often under-utilized. The study highlighted the significance of investing in training and technical product support, and while the technical aspects of a product are important, it is assumed knowledge. Customers truly seek the desired outcome, so why is there so much emphasis placed on the product itself rather than the desired outcome?

According to the study, market share is expected to decline due to increased competition from direct buying and alternative distribution channels. To counter this, the concept of bundling products to reduce soft costs has emerged. This is where the evolution of supply chain management becomes crucial, as it addresses the various hidden costs associated with doing business. The cleaning industry is inherently complex, but by bundling products with fewer distributors, operational costs can be reduced. It is essential to trust the distributor to be an active participant in the cost reduction efforts and to share initiatives aimed at reducing these soft costs. This approach allows for a greater focus on labor solutions, enabling a faster and smarter way to clean and achieve superior outcomes. For those wondering what these soft costs entail, they include activities such as issuing purchase orders, processing payments, managing product movement, maintaining inventory, and allocating shelf space. As a professional salesperson, differentiating yourself through supply chain management and labor reduction for operations is crucial in today's competitive landscape. Competition is emerging from various angles, with outside companies viewing cleaning products as mere add-ons to their orders, solely focused on obtaining a better price. This commoditization of the industry has led to increased competition from external influences. To counter this, it is essential to shift the focus towards finding and embracing the value concept. By doing so, you can overcome margin erosion and increase your commission earnings. Every point of margin contributes to added earnings, making it vital to restore margins and commissions. The emergence of these new competitive channels has downgraded the perception of cleaning products. To differentiate yourself and achieve better results, it is necessary to change your approach and emphasize the value you bring to the table.

Discovering and emphasizing your unique value proposition is key to outshining your competitors. Instead of solely focusing on products due to pricing pressures, consider changing processes for your customers. An excellent example is altering a cleaning process that allows you to earn more commissions while using fewer products. It may sound unconventional, but this approach effectively builds trust in both you and your company. Have you ever heard the saying "sell less and make more"? The true value lies in the labor aspect, not just the product itself. Your emerging competitors are unlikely to invest the time or effort to learn and understand the value concept, particularly when it comes to the labor side. By capitalizing on this opportunity, you can differentiate yourself and gain a competitive edge.

By offering bundled solutions to your customers, you create a significant barrier for competitors to undercut your pricing and potentially lose the account. Customers can easily go online and find the same product at a cheaper price, which could lead them to eliminate you as a vendor. However, they cannot replicate your expertise and knowledge in labor. It is important for the cleaning industry to recognize that large multi-location accounts, such as retail chains, will either opt for national cleaning contractors or purchase directly from manufacturers. The challenge lies in the expanding gray area, where market classifications are increasingly engaging in direct relationships with manufacturers or contractors. This shift, which would have been unimaginable in the past, is evident in sectors like education.

When discussing retail establishments like Walmart, Target, or multi-location stores found in malls, it is surprising to see companies like Staples entering the janitorial business. Many companies that ventured into the janitorial industry as an additional offering soon realized that it was shinny as it appeared. I have yet to come across a successful example. The cleaning industry is often underestimated in terms of its complexity. It is disheartening to see manufacturers squeezing every benefit from distribution channels and seeking further growth, even if it means competing against their own brand in the marketplace.

The study discussed the anticipated growth outlook for the 2000s, highlighting the expectation of flat growth, increased pricing pressure, lower margins, and higher customer expectations for value-added services. However, the study did not clearly define what constitutes value-added services. Instead, it focused more on serving customers with products. In previous chapters, I mentioned the importance of recognizing the value and solution that can differentiate and restore street margins. The study also acknowledged the ever-changing landscape of janitorial supplies and the evolving delivery mechanisms that have occurred over the years. Unfortunately, this change has been driven by the industry's transformation into a commodity. As manufacturers face sales challenges, they often opt for the path of least resistance, further disrupting the distribution channels and contributing to the erosion of their market value.

Over the years, there has been a noticeable slowdown in product innovation within the industry. When I first entered this field forty-two years ago, manufacturers were constantly introducing innovative products that quickly made their way to market through selected distribution channels. However, it is disheartening to see a decline in attendance at trade shows, due to the lack of new and exciting products being produced. Nobody is truly focusing on understanding what clients truly desire-ways to reduce their labor budget. There is still a lack of understanding regarding the impact that certain products can have on labor efficiency. While autonomous cleaning equipment is emerging as a potential solution, it does come with its own setbacks. Issues such as price, reliability, and safety need to be addressed before widespread adoption can occur.

The study highlighted the shift from outside sales to inside sales, which generated a lot of discussion. During my time with the regional distribution company, we also experimented with an inside sales force. We found it to be successful as they were able to reach out to accounts that the outside sales force had overlooked. Although there were occasional conflicts and overlaps, we managed to acquire numerous accounts through this approach. However, the implementation of minimum freight policies in recent times has had a detrimental impact on inside sales programs. Interestingly, the same regional distributor, which has since been acquired by a plumbing company, has now transitioned all their inside salespeople to outside sales roles. I believe this shift has occurred with many pioneering companies across the country. There has been a noticeable shift in mindset towards inside sales, and this can be attributed to the fact that customers are now seeking a comprehensive solution rather than just a product. In the cleaning business, it is important to actively engage with customers in the field to understand their needs and drive cost reduction. Sitting behind a computer screen alone cannot achieve this. The complexities of identifying customer requirements and delivering value are best addressed through direct interaction in the field. This is where the true return on investment lies.

Is the customer becoming reliant on online searches for products, or is the real issue that janitorial suppliers are failing to add value and provide comprehensive solutions? Everything has become commoditized, with an overwhelming focus on price. As a buyer, wouldn't you simply conduct online research and make a purchase if there is nothing more to consider? In the cleaning industry, professional salespeople have the power to change this perception by offering a strong value proposition. Many companies have rebranded their salespeople as consultants or solution providers, but only a few live up to these titles. They fail to actively engage with customers and become part of their cost reduction team, aligning with the initiatives set forth for that year. By actively participating in a customer's cost reduction team, salespeople can transition from selling based on price to selling based on value.

As gross margins decrease, sales commissions follow. Many wholesale distributors have resorted to paying their sales representatives based on a percentage of margin, while some have become frustrated and shifted to a salary-based structure with bonuses tied to achieving specific goals and initiatives. Drawing from my personal experience as a former owner of a janitorial supply company, I can attest to the common mistake of hiring salespeople from within the industry with the expectation of inheriting a customer base. Unfortunately, this often leads to the adoption of bad habits. However, by focusing on niche markets and identifying opportunities to differentiate ourselves and provide added value to customers, we were able to overcome this challenge. The turnover rate for salespeople in this industry is alarmingly high, and it would be beneficial for someone to conduct a study on the significant expenses incurred from hiring the wrong salespeople in wholesale distribution. I must admit that I, too, am guilty of this oversight. During my time as a business owner, I went through several salespeople, and I noticed a common trend: many individuals were not interested in joining as straight, commission-based representatives. Instead, they preferred a salary-based structure. I did have a couple of salespeople on salary, but as soon as I transitioned them to a commission-based model, they quickly left. This experience highlights the importance of making the right decisions when it comes to hiring salespeople. There is a significant cost associated with bringing on a new salesperson, and if they are not adequately trained or educated on selling value, it is unrealistic to expect anything other than a revolving door of turnover. Investing time and effort into training and educating salespeople on the importance of selling value is long-term survival.

As we assess the state of our industry, it is evident that turbulent times lie ahead. Many are wondering how to address the declining margins. I can recall that when I first entered this industry, distribution margins were high 40 percent plus. However, during my tenure at the regional distribution company, they dropped to the 30 percent range. Today, I can confidently say that they have further decreased to the low to mid-twenty percent range, and it is likely that they will soon dip below 20 percent. If I reflect on my time as a distribution company owner, operating at a 20 percent margin would have been unsustainable. The cost of serving customers has increased, their needs have evolved, and the ability to maintain healthy margins has significantly eroded for distributors. On the other hand, manufacturers are preoccupied with finding ways to bypass distribution or explore alternative distribution channels. I anticipate the emergence of a new form of distribution that will offer customers innovative solutions that are challenging for competitors to replicate. In situations of uncertainty, competitors will resort to price as their fallback strategy. However, for these pioneering distributors, street margins will rebound, commissions will increase significantly, and a new breed of professional sales warriors will emerge.

Upon reflecting on this chapter, it becomes evident that while the study had many accurate insights, its timing was premature as many of the predicted changes took longer to materialize. It was intriguing to observe the initial concerns shared by manufacturers and distributors when the study was first published. They dismissed the notion that technology alone could transform the industry and believed that office products would not have a place in our field. The focus seemed to be on continuing to sell products, and the idea of our industry being commoditized was not aligned with their priorities. It was challenging to shift the mindset towards educating salespeople on labor and attracting talented professionals or recent graduates to the industry when the perception was that it was commoditized.

Why would anyone be interested in entering an unchallenging industry? Look around and you will notice that most individuals in this field are older. I have been a part of this industry for forty-two years, and I can attest that this demographic has not changed much over time. The older generation eventually ages out, and they are replaced by more of the same. I am drafting this book to share my perspectives and experiences. I have had a fulfilling career in this industry and would not trade it for anything. I have witnessed numerous changes and learned valuable lessons along the way. I believe that this industry has the potential to thrive, but it needs to make some adjustments. A youth movement is necessary to inject fresh energy and ideas. New recruits need to be challenged and shown that they can achieve financial success. It is imperative to provide them with proper training in selling products based on value rather than just focusing on pricing. Failing to invest time and effort in engaging with millennials will result in their quick disillusionment, leading to high turnover rates and unexpected expenses. The industry is currently struggling to establish its identity, and it is unfortunate that more companies have not undergone a complete transformation to attract young sales professionals. Without significant changes, it will only become more challenging to attract and retain talent in this industry.

Lessons Learned

- Data and information can serve as valuable resources to fuel businesses.

- Predictions and unsupported speculation can be accurate, inaccurate, or remain uncertain in terms of timing and occurrences.

- It is essential to anticipate changing trends and proactively plan for them.

- Embrace the future and plan for it without fear.

- We are in an industry that is often undervalued, but we should take pride in the fact that we are all cleaning professionals.

CHAPTER 6

CATCHING THE PACIFIC WAVE

I assumed the role of president in a well-established manufacturing company in 1998, based in Muskegon, Michigan, with a rich history spanning seventy-five years. Originally founded in the Bay Area, the company was under the ownership of a remarkable individual named Sam, who prioritized the development of top-notch floor machines within the cleaning industry. Subsequently, Larry, the president of Clarke floor machine, whom I had the pleasure of meeting during my initial training visit back in 1980, acquired Sam's company. This marked the beginning of a series of acquisitions that would follow the Hines Corporation. It was during this time that I had the privilege of learning from my third mentor, Larry, a successful business entrepreneur and financial expert whose guidance proved to be invaluable.

Despite encountering obstacles, such as Brenda's reluctance to relocate, I decided to maintain an apartment in the new location for a span of eight years. This allowed me to commute back and forth between my family and work. When people inquired about the distance of my drive, I would respond with, "Three hours and forty-seven minutes door-to-door." We made this sacrifice and commitment to ensure our children's education remained uninterrupted, as they were enrolled in one of the highest-rated schools in the Midwest.

As I embarked on my journey to Muskegon, my primary objective was to familiarize myself with the staff, both in the office and the plant. Over time, these individuals not only became trusted business associates but also formed lasting friendships. Initially, I prioritized gaining a comprehensive understanding of the company, its employees, culture, goals, and aspirations. It became evident that everyone shared a burning desire to succeed. Armed with this knowledge, I dedicated a week to crafting my business plan. The creation of a forty-five-page comprehensive plan provided us with a clear roadmap to navigate. Our objective was straightforward: how could we increase our market share using the current line of equipment we produced? As a smaller company operating in a mature market with numerous equipment manufacturers, innovation was key to establishing our presence. While the saying, "if you build it, they will come" holds some truth, it was merely the initial step in our mission. To effectively bring our innovations to the market, we recognized the need for a highly motivated sales force.

During my first week in the new position, I conducted a thorough assessment of our sales force using an evaluation system I had developed over the years. To my dismay, our team scored a mere thirty-five out of one hundred on the rating scale. Recognizing the need for improvement, I directed our sales managers, Paul and Bob, to actively search for ambitious and financially driven salespeople within the industry. It was important to strike a balance between implementing necessary changes and providing guidance to our associates during this period of rapid turnover. I aimed to avoid being perceived as a leader who made hasty decisions or functioned as a "hatchet man." However, it was evident that we needed to enhance our team with individuals who possessed expertise in equipment, strong industry contacts, and a drive to achieve financial success. Within twelve months, I conducted another evaluation, and the changes we made resulted in a representation that brought us closer to a 68 percent score. This marked a significant improvement in our field representation. It became evident that having the right personnel in the right positions could truly make a difference.

The next aspect I needed to evaluate was our engineering staff's willingness to embrace the development of new and innovative equipment outlined in the plan. While the team consisted of talented individuals, they were nearing the end of their careers and had experienced significant success working with Larry at Clarke. To infuse fresh perspectives and ideas, we decided to hire a young engineer from a different industry to join our engineering team. Together, we collaborated on several equipment projects. Additionally, I opted to outsource certain projects to a reputable design engineer who had previously worked with Clarke. This engineer, Tom, served as a consultant and had established close relationships with many individuals within our organization. Prior to my arrival, another associate Larry had brought over from Clarke, Bob, had conceived the idea of a mini edger designed to clean baseboards and hard-to-reach areas. It was akin to a weed whacker for cleaning purposes. The product proved to be a resounding success, filling a niche in the industry. Two notable projects stand out in my memory, both of which significantly boosted our business. The first innovation was the introduction of a wide-area vacuum equipped with a twenty-five foot retractable hose, allowing for efficient cleaning of stairs and high-dust areas with a single machine. The second breakthrough was the development of the industry's first battery backpack. We demonstrated a rough prototype of this product at the 1999 industry trade show. To put our forward-thinking into perspective, competitors did not introduce battery backpacks to the market until 2003. In the realm of manufacturing and innovation, the only way to gain a competitive advantage and capture market share is by thinking creatively and continuously innovating. Stagnation and adhering to the status quo will not lead to growth.

During my tenure, I made it a point to regularly walk the plant floor and establish personal connections with everyone. One memory stands out: the challenge match with Betty, who oversaw the floor machine production line. During a company luncheon, I jokingly told Betty that I believed I could produce a machine faster than her. The group chuckled, but to my surprise, Betty immediately accepted the challenge, exclaiming, "That's called a challenge match!" We set a date and prepared for the showdown. However, Betty outperformed me by a wide margin. As I struggled to keep up, I observed the camaraderie and enjoyment among the team as they cheered for Betty's impressive speed. I was soundly defeated. Yet, this experience taught me a valuable lesson: make time in business to have fun and appreciate one another's company.

Early on, I investigated rebranding, which comes with its fair share of complexities. I vividly remember the Atlanta show. We were excited to unveil our new logo and color scheme, hoping to display our fresh identity. However, to our disappointment, the show turned out to be a complete flop with minimal attendance. It was one of the worst shows in the industry's history. This experience taught me that changing a brand requires time and a collective effort from everyone involved to make a lasting impact. Unfortunately, we did not execute it properly, and our new logo and brand failed to resonate with our audience. The complexities I mentioned earlier, particularly in producing various color components, added to the challenges we faced. Considering we already had a mix of private labels, we decided to reverse our decision before investing excessive effort and money. This experience taught me a valuable lesson: changing a brand is a significant undertaking that requires the full commitment of the entire team. If there is not widespread buy-in, it's best not to expend energy on it. Additionally, I was surprised to discover that our marketing firm had not protected our tag line, allowing a competitor who had found success in the residential market to steal it upon entering the commercial business. This incident highlighted the need for an ethics code in business and reinforced the importance of trademarking everything to safeguard intellectual property.

International Exposure

To complete our product line, I sought assistance from other original equipment manufacturers (OEMs). To accomplish this, I attended an industry show in Europe, where I had the opportunity to connect with numerous companies offering unique equipment. During that time, European companies were at the forefront of auto scrubber manufacturing. To expedite our entry into the market, I conducted extensive research to identify companies capable of providing private label machines. Fortunately, Charlie, a former colleague from earlier in my career, assisted me in making introductions.

Auto scrubbers were known for their high revenue generation potential. Eventually, we formed partnerships with two Italian companies that played a crucial role in rounding out our product line. One relationship that stands out in my memory is with Oswaldo, an industry legend who owned a successful manufacturing company. Not only did we collaborate professionally, but we also developed a close friendship, enjoying memorable moments with his family and business associates. He possessed a background in engineering and harbored a deep passion for the cleaning industry. With two sons who continued his legacy, they made strategic shifts in the company's direction that proved successful. Ale spearheaded the transformation, turning the business into an industrial powerhouse.

I fondly remember a memorable evening with Oswaldo, dining at Trattoria Cammillo, a restaurant in Florence, Italy, engaging in discussions about international business and our community. As we enjoyed multiple glasses of wine and a delicious dinner, our conversation turned to the need for a vacuum that could rival the top-selling units in the market. We began sketching out the concept on a napkin, fueled by our shared vision. Several weeks later, Oswaldo sent over the design layout drawings of the vacuum, marking the first tangible evidence of two visionary individuals-a skilled engineer and an enthusiastic salesman-coming together to innovate and improve. Our friendship endured for many years, and Oswaldo would often commend my tenacity at trade shows, remarking on my unparalleled dedication to working the booth and demonstrating our products.

Innovation begets further innovation. As the years went by, I could not help but feel that the vacuum industry needed a meaningful change. This realization struck me in the early 2000s. I conceptualized a vacuum design where the vacuum system would be housed in the base, while the hose would be integrated into the handle. This unique configuration allowed the hose to detach from the base, enabling efficient cleaning of corners, stairs, and upholstery. Although I cannot recall the specific project name, it had the potential to be a game-changer. Today, if we observe the residential vacuum market, we can see similar concepts being implemented. Unfortunately, we chose not to pursue this innovation due to the exorbitant upfront costs and the associated risks. We lacked the knowledge and resources to bring such a product to fruition, so we opted to stick with what we were familiar with. In hindsight, it was a missed opportunity that I now recognize.

While on my way to an industrial trade show, I came across a manual sweeper from Germany that immediately caught my attention. The company's general manager, Michael, was overseeing the product. Recognizing its potential in the American market, I proposed a partnership, and our company began selling twin disk manual sweepers. The innovation lay in the patented wheels that activated the brushes as the machine was pushed forward. I vividly remember reaching out to QVC regarding a unit specifically designed for residential use, inquiring if they would be interested in featuring it on their channel. One thing led to another, and before I knew it, I was flying to Philadelphia to demonstrate the machine on live television. Upon arrival, I met the host of our segment, who kindly advised me to refrain from using any profanity or behaving out of character, as the show was broadcasted live, and nothing would be edited. Our demonstration took place outside a simulated house in the driveway in front of the garage. The host instructed me to place debris on the driveway for the demonstration. I gathered leaves, pinecones, and litter to demonstrate the effectiveness of the machine. The host directed my attention to a display that resembled a twenty-four-second clock in basketball. She explained that it would show the number of units sold during the three-minute time limit. With lights, camera, and action, the demonstration began. The machine effortlessly picked up everything in a single pass. As I glanced over at the display, the numbers rapidly climbed: three hundred, four hundred, five hundred, six hundred, seven hundred, eight hundred. We finally stopped at 808 machines sold. It was an impressive result for just three minutes. This experience holds a special place in my heart and continues to be a source of laughter and fond memories among my colleagues.

The opening of trade doors with China presented an opportunity for many manufacturers to reduce costs for their products. However, during my trips to China in search of the right solution for my company, I could not help but notice a stark contrast in ethical considerations and principles. Sitting in meetings, I found myself grappling with the dilemma of navigating business practices in this context. All notions of ethics and principles were disregarded when dealing with Chinese counterparts. It became evident that they would swiftly replicate machines or copy patented components before you even left the building. Witnessing the working conditions and the meager wages these individuals endured while producing products was disheartening. It was a regrettable situation where greed corrupted everything. US companies, driven solely by the desire for increased profits, appeared to ignore these ethical concerns.

We had a sister company involved in the pump business, and they had a plant in China. It seemed like the most logical step to begin producing a few of our floor machines there and assess the outcome. It was disheartening to realize that, to compete in the American market, we had to rely on manufacturing in China. The quality of the machines varied, with some lacking the desired standards and others exhibiting imperfections. We continued this arrangement for several years before ultimately deciding to bring production back to the United States. At that point, we had to make a major decision: whether to further engage in the commonization of the equipment industry or take a different approach by prioritizing American quality.

I have had numerous experiences with Chinese businesspeople, and one thing that stands out is their penchant for heavy drinking and smoking. I distinctly remember hosting a Chinese company in Muskegon, where we took them to a popular restaurant. Curious about their smoking policy, I inquired if they could smoke inside. They responded that it was not really allowed, but they had a separate room where they could accommodate us, away from other patrons. As we sat down, I was taken aback by the sight of around twenty packs of cigarettes on the table. The smoke quickly filled the room, making it difficult to see the person sitting across from me. It's hard to imagine requesting such a concession in today's times. Another memorable experience was when I flew into Hong Kong for the first time, before taking a train to the factories inland. I struck up a conversation with a lady sitting next to me on the plane. When I mentioned that I needed to rent a car upon landing, she looked at me with wide eyes and advised against it, saying it was the last thing I should do. Trusting her advice, I opted for a cab instead. As I looked out from the cab, I deeply appreciated the wisdom of her words. Firstly, driving on the right side of the vehicle, following British rule, added to the sense of chaos on the roads. It felt like an accident waiting to happen for me. I had the opportunity to try various cultural foods, some of which I may never eat again. Surprisingly, the snake dish was quite enjoyable and tasted like chicken. Many US companies saw business opportunities in China as a necessity. Personally, I didn't prioritize building relationships or engaging in business dealings there. However, it made me reflect on the potential impact if these companies had invested the same efforts and resources domestically. By avoiding the devaluation of products, which led to lower street prices, we could have prevented the commoditization of the cleaning industry that we face today. The Chinese market's influence has forced many to compete solely on price. If it's not China, another country will emerge with manufacturing plants. In the future, "Sell and buy American" may become a permanent fixture in the fabric of American commerce.

Importing products is often necessary when a company lacks the capability to produce them internally. Cost reduction is another motivation, especially when innovative minds are lacking. While I acknowledge the importance of considering material costs, it is important to explore alternative methods of cost reduction without compromising quality. It's essential to recognize that our actions today have consequences for future generations. Unfortunately, the prevailing mindset often prioritizes short-term gains over long-term sustainability. The focus tends to be on maximizing profits in the present, with little regard for the impact on tomorrow.

As we explored opportunities to expand our international distribution, the Russian market caught my attention. I came across a gentleman named Leon, who specialized in coordinating international partnerships in Russia. Intrigued by the potential, I decided to visit Russia to gain firsthand insight into their janitorial distribution landscape. It became apparent that they purchased equipment from European suppliers. While we were able to conduct some business, the distance proved to be a challenge for sustained operations. However, my trip to Moscow was a fascinating experience. My driver, a former military agent, was friendly and picked me up from the airport, taking me to the flat where I was staying. The exterior of the apartments resembled the slums of Brooklyn, but upon entering, I was greeted by lavish living quarters. Each morning, we indulged in vodka, caviar, and eggs before I set out to visit the distributors. These distributors managed and operated their companies similarly to their counterparts elsewhere, with one notable difference: corruption and payoffs were prevalent in their business practices.

The night before my departure back to the States, I received an invitation to meet with the largest building service contractor in Russia, along with his wife and their friends, at Club Moscow. The nightclub was an interesting experience, filled with smoking, drinking, and a lively atmosphere. Afterward, I was invited to their apartment in a high-rise building that offered a stunning view of the city. We gathered around, engaging in conversations about our respective cultures and the cleaning industry. At one point, the contractor suggested switching from vodka to scotch, and we continued drinking well into the early morning hours. It was then that his wife and the other wives at the table reminded me of my 7:00 a.m. flight, as it was already 3:30 a.m.. Time had flown by as we enjoyed each other's company and laughed at the differences between our countries. Realizing it was time for me to leave, they asked for my opinion on Russian women. I jokingly replied that they all appeared to have disciplined workout routines. On my return flight, I noticed an unexpectedly substantial number of babies onboard, highlighting the significant cultural exchange taking place. It was an eye-opening experience that left an impression. Moscow stood out as a stunningly beautiful city. I had the privilege of exploring many of its historical landmarks and immersing myself in the rich culture of the country.

Relentless Night Rider

Back in the States, I have a memorable story that perfectly exemplifies pure grit and determination. We caught the attention of a national contractor who was interested in our equipment line. Tom, the VP of operations, had scheduled all his supervisors to meet us at a Target store in Toledo, Ohio, a store they were cleaning. We were going to be demonstrating our Center Fire propane cleaning systems. However, I found myself on the East Coast conducting distributor meetings and visiting Triple-S. As I made my way towards the ticket counter, someone informed me that I wouldn't be able to leave that day due to an approaching hurricane (Hurricane Floyd). This was early afternoon, and I needed to be back for the meetings and demonstrations at 6:00 a.m. that next morning. In a moment of quick thinking, I decided to rent a car. I grabbed the rental car and began my journey westward. It was a ten-hour drive, and if I didn't encounter any further issues, I could make it to the meeting on time. So, I drove for ten hours straight, determined to reach my destination. One amusing detail I often share with others is that I was so focused on my goal that I didn't even put on my seat belt. The seat belt alarm rang for nine hours and fifteen minutes, but I was determined to wear it out. I eventually stopped at a hotel and asked the receptionist if I could pay for just forty-five minutes. She laughed, but I insisted that I only needed a shower and shave. After about forty-five minutes, I got back in the car, and just before I arrived, the seat belt alarm finally died. As I stepped out of my car, I saw everyone waiting outside the retail location, including the president of the contractor. He asked, "Weren't you out East?" I confidently replied, "Yes, but not even a hurricane could prevent me from being here." He was astonished and asked, "You mean you drove all night?" I responded, "Absolutely. I wouldn't miss this opportunity."

Throughout my time in the industry, one consistent theme emerged: my relationship with the Triple-S Association. Our company proudly served as a key supplier, offering a private label line of equipment for Triple-S. This association remained a hub for premier distribution companies across the country. Together, we experienced remarkable growth and achieved profitable outcomes. It is worth noting that Sam, the previous owner of Pacific, played a crucial role in nurturing this relationship. Despite Larry's insistence that Sam remain active in the company, he was still with us when we were honored with the prestigious Supplier of the Year award. The association was filled with exceptional individuals who played a significant part in our journey. As you continue reading, you will witness in the proceeding chapters how this relationship continued to flourish and take on an important role in my entrepreneurial quest.

Our company's relentless drive, determination, and commitment to innovation began to garner attention within the industry. By expanding our product line and focusing on new product development, we found the perfect formula to rapidly double our size. We were starting to draw attention from larger companies in the retail and commercial business.

Where were you when 9/11 happened? I remember being in a boardroom meeting when our controller entered and informed us that the towers were on fire. Immediately, our attention shifted to the television screen, and the scene unfolding before us felt surreal. Little did we know the profound impact it would have on countless lives. As a New Yorker, I was filled with anger and frustration. The perpetrators had succeeded in their goal of taking American lives and crippling the economy. Most businesses, including ours, experienced a significant downturn for the next twelve-eighteen months. However, it was the brave individuals who lost their lives, the families left behind, and the resilient citizens of New York who bore the brunt of the tragedy. It was a stark reminder that we can never truly anticipate when something unimaginable might occur. We must never forget the events of that day and the lives that were forever changed.

After the 9/11 tragedy, the economy faced significant challenges, and the focus on capital goods diminished. To counter the revenue decline, we had to explore alternative avenues. Taking initiative, I contacted the Hoover Company and arranged a meeting with their executive team to discuss their commercial/institutional division. During the meeting, I inquired about their growth plans for that division, considering they already owned the retail business at the time.

Recognizing an opportunity, I presented Pacific as a potential partner, highlighting the expertise of our independent reps across the company who could effectively handle both product lines. After negotiations, we reached a mutually beneficial agreement where Pacific would not only handle both lines but also manage their national account business. This collaboration proved to be successful for both companies, allowing us to leverage our strengths and drive growth in the market.

The decision to expand our partnership with the Hoover Company was a strategic move that helped us navigate the economic challenges post-9/11. By diversifying our offerings and capitalizing on our existing resources, we were able to create a win-win situation that propelled both companies forward.

Overall, this new project brought about positive outcomes, strengthening our position in the market, and fostering a fruitful relationship with the Hoover Company. It serves as a testament to the power of collaboration and adaptability in overcoming obstacles and finding new avenues for success.

As our business began to recover, I could not shake the restlessness I felt. I started contemplating a "what if" scenario: What if I could start my own company from scratch? The constant travel was taking a toll on me, and my family longed for more quality time together. So, I began dedicating my evenings to crafting a business plan. This plan surpassed any previous plans I had created for the current company. Drawing from my extensive financial experience, leveraging my past sales, and marketing knowledge, I developed a comprehensive plan that instilled confidence and could be presented to any bank. I was prepared to put everything on the line-refinancing the house, utilizing my 401K, securing a bank loan-fueled by sheer determination. While Brenda initially thought I was crazy, she could not ignore my record. It is true that 70 percent of start-ups fail, but I knew deep down that I had the drive and skills to make it a success. When I shared my intentions with Larry, he expressed his belief that if anyone could make it successful, it would be me. His vote of confidence meant a great deal, coming from a man who had built an empire of companies. Entrepreneurship was in my blood, and I felt compelled to venture out and pursue it.

Lessons Learned

- It is important to prioritize having fun and appreciating each other's company in business.
- Taking risks is an integral aspect of any accomplished entrepreneur's trajectory.
- Trademark everything to safeguard intellectual property.
- Failure can be a catalyst for growth, as it imparts valuable lessons.
- Refusing to succumb to fear of failure means avoiding a stagnant existence and settling for mediocrity.
- Exceptional leaders persevere and continuously strive for success, undeterred by setbacks.

CHAPTER 7

LEVERAGE EVERYTHING

I recall the exhaustion I felt as I sat in my car, waiting for a 10:00 a.m. meeting with the operations department at a prestigious university. Securing an appointment with the facilities director had been a challenging task. I remember dozing off in my car, desperately hoping to wake up in time. It was a stroke of luck when one of the facility cleaners tapped on my window to inform me that I was parked in someone else's spot. Thanks to his timely intervention, I made it to the meeting, which turned out to be highly advantageous as they eventually became a valuable customer of mine.

Starting your own business is exciting, challenging, nerve-racking, tiring, and a huge financial risk. It is critical to approach it systematically, especially when establishing a new brand in the market. In my case, I chose the name Intelligent Cleaning Systems for my company and centered the brand around floor-care systems and solutions. I recognized that floor-care sales required significant time and effort, but I also understood that most customers preferred quick results. Therefore, my focus was on putting in the work and earning their trust. Initially, I had no intention of venturing into the consumable business, which typically involves high volume but low profit margins. However, as customers witnessed the impressive results I achieved on their floors, they began to inquire if I also supplied janitorial supplies. I responded affirmatively, and they expressed their desire to purchase everything from me. This experience taught me a valuable lesson: by starting with the more challenging sales aspect, I was ultimately rewarded with the easier part of the business, which came with higher profit margins.

I created a comprehensive eighty-nine-page business plan that played a crucial role in securing the business loan and Triple-S agreement. Triple-S has members across the country with exceptional brand acceptance and regional distribution centers, providing members inventory replenishment. In the following paragraphs, I will provide condensed advice based on the plan.

The inspiration to start my own business came from my urge to be challenged and hearing many share their thoughts on a start-up company being a likely failure. When I started crafting the business plan, it became essential to effectively convey my vision to the reader in a simple yet convincing manner. My executive summary successfully achieved this by highlighting the actual opportunity at hand. It clearly outlined what my company was prepared to do differently from competitors. I made sure to provide a concise and accurate description of the business, its products, and services in comparison to other competitive companies. Additionally, the summary included the financial potential and concluded with a clear request. Essentially, the goal is to ask for the order, loan, or agreement with confidence.

The subsequent section of the business plan addressed the suppliers, products, the process of securing credit, and how inventory management and turnover would be handled. This section is important as it covers the competitive landscape and the products that would be shared in the market. I refer to this as "share selling" because it typically implies lower margins or returns. However, I also had the advantage of the Triple-S brand, which was my own brand. This private label represented higher margins and superior returns, setting it apart from the shared selling products.

I had a clear definition of the industry, competition, and market in the plan. This was supported by documentation that explained the competitive landscape, the actual market size, and the market potential. Additionally, it was important to outline customer profiles and identify the type of customers I intended to pursue.

When describing the services offered, I ensured that the scope was broad enough for the reader to understand the infrastructure that would be in place to support and sustain growth. This gave them a comprehensive view of how the company planned to meet the needs of its customers and established a strong foundation for future success.

The sales and marketing plan was aligned with our competitive advantage, pricing principles, customer channels, promotional strategies, and most importantly, our customer feedback system. This feedback system served as a measurement tool to ensure that we were adhering to the plan and following the prioritized steps.

In addition, we had a well-crafted operational plan that included the location of the warehouse and offices, facility layout, operational capital equipment expenses, suppliers' logistics, personnel plan, and general operations flow. To enhance clarity and understanding, I utilized flow charts extensively in my plan. These flow charts provided a simple and visual representation of the operational processes, making it easier for to follow and comprehend.

The management section of the business plan encompassed the organizational structure, ownership details, and key management principles. It was important to provide a detailed organizational chart that outlined the roles and responsibilities of each associate. If there was a need for outside services, such as industry consultants, it was essential to clearly tie them to an expense and provide justification for the benefits gained from investing in those areas. Additionally, I included the board of directors, and their résumés to showcase their qualifications and expertise.

The goals and strategies section of the business plan clearly aligned with action plans to achieve them. It was crucial to demonstrate how these strategies would support the growth of top-line revenues and contribute to overall success. Additionally, it was important to define the top five keys to success and prioritize them, accordingly, assigning value to each component. This prioritization was essential for the plan to succeed.

Furthermore, it was necessary to go beyond the standard three-year financial projections and provide the reader with a vision of future opportunities with the company. I included discussing potential expansion plans, new markets to explore, and innovative products or services that could be introduced. By presenting a forward-thinking perspective, I showcased the long-term potential and growth prospects of the business.

The financial assumptions section was a major component in any business plan. I included a detailed financial overview supported by documentation, such as three-year revenue projections, start-up costs, profit and loss statements, balance sheets, and ratio analysis. These documents provided a comprehensive understanding of the financial aspects of the business and demonstrated the viability and potential profitability of the venture.

In addition to financial documents, support documents played a key role in achieving the plan. These included my résumé, detailed job descriptions that supported the plan, short-and long-term goals and objectives, measurement tools, profit plan format, frequency of meetings, market segmentation by customer, supplier programs, and any industry-supported differentiation. These support documents provided additional context and evidence to strengthen my plan and showcased the preparedness and strategic thinking.

When starting a business, it is pivotal to carefully consider the initial investment in inventory. In my case, I recognized the significance of the Triple-S Association's regional distribution warehouses and how they could contribute to establishing our brand. To ensure a high turnover rate, I made strategic decisions regarding the inventory mix. However, I also had to address the corporate policy of the Triple-S Association regarding start-ups. Historically, they had not added any new start-up members. In a meeting with them, I presented my impressive business plan and market approach, highlighting the mutual benefits we could gain. As a result, they were impressed and saw the opportunity for both parties. This led to a positive outcome, as they did not have representation in the Indianapolis market and partnering with me would fill that gap. The regional distribution center played a major role in the success of my Greenfield start-up. I vividly remember the early days of my company when pallets of products would arrive from the RDC. Looking at those pallets, I realized the importance of swiftly moving the merchandise. Fortunately, most of those products were already sold, allowing for an immediate turnaround on inventory. This partnership with the association proved to be instrumental in achieving an impressive inventory turnover rate of eighteen times per year. Their contribution was invaluable to the growth and profitability of my business.

After successfully securing the agreement with Triple-S, the next step was to arrange a meeting with the bank. I reached out to a few banking executives, including one whom I knew personally, to provide them with a comprehensive overview of the cleaning industry and the potential opportunities for a small start-up like mine. Drawing upon my executive management experience and track record, I was able to establish a strong and mutually beneficial banking relationship. Securing a business loan was essential to obtaining the necessary capital for launching and operating the company. Following the loan agreement, the bank recommended an accounting firm that would provide valuable assistance with money management, further enhancing the financial aspect of my business.

I arranged a meeting with the accounting firm to discuss my business plan and explore how we could collaborate effectively, including discussing their fees. It was important to establish a solid foundation for our working relationship, which included incorporating my company. During the meeting, I shared my business plan with the firm's team. To my delight, the CEO of the firm said that in all his years of reviewing business plans, mine was the best he had ever seen. The team also commented on how my plan provided a detailed roadmap for success, allowing them to visualize how it would work. They offered valuable suggestions and ideas, which I promptly implemented to ensure compliance and to further enhance the plan's effectiveness.

The following meeting on my agenda was with the new landlord. It was imperative to find a centrally located industrial park for my business, and after careful consideration, I chose the city of Westfield. The space we secured consisted of approximately 15,000 square feet, which included both warehouse and office areas. To keep expenses manageable, I recognized the advantage of utilizing Triple-S and the local master distributors. Therefore, it was important to allocate most of the space to the warehouse, ensuring efficient product receiving and shipping processes. Office space was not a top priority, so we opted for three small offices that provided ample room for our daily work activities.

Next on my agenda were capital investments that were essential for the operation and servicing of customers. I needed a full-service van for demonstration purposes and shipping smaller quantities of products to customers. Additionally, I sought a used forklift to facilitate the receiving of incoming shipments, as well as purchased service tools for minor service and repair work. These investments were critical for our operations and ensuring customer satisfaction.

However, I had to find a solution for product delivery without initially investing in a box truck. Through networking and inquiries, I came across a gentleman named Dave who owned a box truck and provided delivery services for other companies. We arranged a lunch meeting to discuss the opportunity and his financial requirements to commit to the partnership. After reasonable negotiations, we reached an agreement, and Dave became ICS's outsourced delivery partner. This collaboration allowed us to meet our delivery needs efficiently and effectively. Each morning, Dave would arrive promptly at around 7:00 a.m., and we would load him up with the necessary products for deliveries. He would hit the road and complete his deliveries by mid-afternoon. Initially, the pace was slow, but thanks to my unwavering drive and determination to make this project a success, things quickly gained momentum.

In addition to partnering with Triple-S, I quickly established relationships with two master distributors in the city. To expand our supplier network and complement Triple-S, I conducted interviews with various suppliers. However, being a start-up company, many suppliers were skeptical and hesitant to work with us, unsure if we would succeed. Little did they know that they would eventually come knocking on our door.

In the meantime, to meet our immediate needs, I utilized the portfolio of suppliers provided by Triple-S to develop the market. Every six months, I conducted product rationalization to determine which products were essential for differentiating our company. It was interesting to observe how servicing those suppliers benefited us in the long run. It became apparent that those suppliers who initially passed on us quickly realized the value of our business and sought to collaborate with us.

My business plan heavily focused on floor care, specifically stone care restoration and maintenance. Many of my competitors avoided this area due to their lack of experience and fear of damaging floors. To overcome this challenge, I sought to acquire knowledge promptly. Fortunately, I connected with two seasoned veterans in the stone care industry. They generously dedicated their time to teaching me everything they knew, and as a result, I quickly became an expert in the field. Armed with this newfound knowledge, I fearlessly tackled floor-related challenges in the marketplace that my competitors were hesitant to approach.

The upcoming pages in this chapter are dedicated to sharing my customer experiences and how creative thinking, along with a positive attitude, can rapidly grow your business. I found great success by tapping into the local chapter of IEHA, which not only provided me with an instant customer base but also allowed me to voice my ideas and secure significant healthcare business as a member. Later in this chapter, I will delve into some of the long-term relationships I have formed through this invaluable opportunity.

My initial goal was to make a strong start and achieve tangible results. To accomplish this, I conducted thorough research on flooring distributors and installers. Recognizing the potential of partnering with a flooring distributor, I saw it as an excellent opportunity to reach a wider audience. Together, we brainstormed strategies to mutually benefit each other. The flooring company also had a service division that catered to customers' initial investments, which aligned perfectly with our objectives. We devised a program that not only ensured successful outcomes but also secured long-term flooring business. They became a valuable customer, and I am grateful to them for being my first sale.

I vividly remember that day. I had the opportunity to sit down with the manager of the flooring company and discuss the advantages of speed stripping. As we conversed, he glanced at me and said, "Send me a couple of pails, and we'll evaluate." That simple interaction marked the beginning of our fruitful partnership. They quickly became a valued customer, and through their support, I was introduced to numerous other customers in the industry.

I was determined to find a building service contractor that I could collaborate with, as they had a client base I could tap into. My goal was to secure a significant partnership, one that had a prestigious reputation and a strong presence in the downtown area. I recall a meeting with the president and the VP of operations as they passed through Westfield on their way to a PGA tournament in Wisconsin. Over lunch, we discussed how I could contribute to their business by offering services and opportunities that their current supplier had failed to provide. Through my research, I discovered that the incumbent supplier did not offer any compensation to the contractor for recommending consumables to their Class A realtors, despite it being a substantial volume of business. Curious, I asked Tim, the president, about the compensation they received for bringing in such significant business. He turned to the operations manager, Jerry, and inquired if they were receiving any benefits for incorporating consumables into their business operations. He responded with a "no." In response, I proposed the idea of offering them a 15 percent cash justified discount (CJD) on all consumables if they were to switch over to me. Tim looked at me, intrigued, and asked if I was genuinely willing to provide such an adjustment. Without hesitation, I assured him that I was prepared to do so immediately. To estimate the potential volumes based on their clientele list, I collaborated with my consumables suppliers and factored in a 10 percent offset in my offering. Essentially, it would cost me 5 percent to make a significant breakthrough. Tim expressed his interest in discussing the transition upon their return. He expressed frustration with the current supplier's lack of willingness to assist with handling costs. That day, the door swung wide open, earning me a place on their team. I began working closely with their organization to drive out the incumbent supplier, successfully becoming an integral part of their team. This achievement truly put me on the map.

I had to maintain a relentless pace to secure customers and keep my business thriving. There was no time for rest. During the first six months of running my company, I can recall sleeping in a recliner to avoid waking Brenda and children. I was working tirelessly, putting in sixteen-to -eighteen hours a day, actively prospecting for new business and ensuring that the initial investment would yield quick returns. One person who made a lasting impression on me was Hector, a military man associated with a large contractor for whom I had just won the consumables contract. He approached me and asked, "Hey, Bill, do you turn off your phone at 6:00 p.m. in the evening?" He proceeded to advise me to keep my phone active throughout the night because in the contracting world, issues often arise during evening hours. He emphasized that if I truly wanted to expand my business, I should be available to work with them in the evenings, as that's when they typically operated. Following his advice, I found that working with them during those hours significantly increased my business opportunities. Throughout my extensive experience in this industry, I find it ironic how many people choose to shut off their phones at 6:00 p.m. I have learned a valuable lesson from Hector's candid advice; it is crucial not to miss out on opportunities by turning off my phone. I expressed my gratitude to Hector for enlightening me with this insight. As I moved forward, I discovered that a significant portion of my future business was conducted in the evenings. During this time, I conducted demos and worked on finding solutions for frontline workers, while my competitors were asleep. This strategic approach allowed me to seize opportunities that others might have overlooked.

For four consecutive months, I diligently called a potential customer every Friday morning, leaving voicemails without receiving any return calls. However, I was determined to connect with him. One day, I decided to switch up my routine and get creative. Using a different phone, I called him at 11:45 a.m., just before lunchtime. To my surprise, he answered the call and upon recognizing my voice, he burst into laughter. He remarked, "Man, you just don't know how to take no for an answer; you never give up." I responded by highlighting the potential opportunities he might be missing out on if he didn't hear me out. In response, he proposed a deal; he would give me thirty minutes of his time the following Tuesday, on the condition that I stopped the regimented Friday morning calls. I gladly accepted the offer, and true to his word, we met the following week. Not only did he become one of my valued customers, but we also developed a strong friendship.

I developed a strong passion and achieved considerable success in the higher education sector. I actively engaged with facility managers on numerous sales opportunities, appreciating their focus on seeking value-added solutions. Given their substantial workforce, they prioritized labor reductions, making it a key objective for them.

I stumbled upon another opportunity with a prominent university due to the lackadaisical approach of a competitor. My contact was facing difficulties with her current suppliers in designing a recycling program. Curious about their reluctance, she expressed her dissatisfaction. Sensing an opening, I offered to assist and requested the program requirements. Assuring her that I would collaborate with my can liner company, I promised to deliver a tailored program within a week. This proactive approach paid off as I successfully secured the business, fulfilling a long-held aspiration. Truckloads of products were drop-shipped, with the high-volume liners contributing to increased revenues and impressive margins. This experience serves as a prime example of the rewards reaped by going the extra mile. Although it wasn't easy to meet her requirements, I worked closely with the vendor to make it happen. I enjoyed the business for three years, thanks to a binding agreement that ensured its continuity. This highlights a common issue among salespeople who fail to protect their solutions with such agreements, often leading to their being taken for granted.

I hired my first sales representative, Kim, to oversee the southern Indiana market. He successfully brought in some business for our company. Kim proved to be an invaluable employee and a close friend, as we shared both challenging and rewarding moments together. He had connections within a major university that had a long-standing contract, which I had initially established while working for a regional powerhouse. When the university invited only four companies to bid, I was pleasantly surprised to discover that we performed exceptionally well as a small company, as indicated by the RFP recap. However, the university's response was disheartening, as they believed we were too small to handle the business. Despite this disappointment, it served as a valuable learning experience for us. Kim continued to cultivate a strong customer base in southern Indiana, contributing to the growth of our company.

After two years, I recall one day Dave and I searching for a specific product in our overcrowded warehouse. Pallets were stacked so closely together that we had to carefully navigate on top of them. In that moment, we shared a laugh and acknowledged that it was time for a new warehouse. Conducting business in such cramped conditions was no longer sustainable. This incident served as a true testament to the hard work we had put in to meet our customers' needs, and it was clear that our efforts were paying off. Determined to improve our operations, I began searching for a larger warehouse, aiming to double our space and introduce efficient racking systems. Eventually, I found a suitable location in Westfield, and we embarked on the challenging process of moving everything to the new facility. It goes without saying that relocating warehouses is no easy feat.

As the business experienced rapid growth, it became evident that it was time to bring the driving and operations in-house. With recommendations from Dave, I interviewed several candidates and came across a promising young man named Eric. He would be responsible for driving and managing the warehouse. Prior to this, I had been handling everything myself. My typical day consisted of a minimum of five to six sales calls, scheduling three to four trucks during lunch, making bank deposits, and making one or two late deliveries in the afternoon or early evening for contractors. While Dave took care of driving the truck, I handled all other aspects of the business. This is the reality one signs up for when starting one's own business-being prepared to roll up your sleeves and work harder than ever imagined, ensuring its success.

When we purchased our first box truck, it was an exciting moment for us. The truck was brand new and had a clean white exterior. We knew that to reach a wider audience, we needed to find a way to advertise our message effectively. After considering various options, we decided to go for a full wrap on the truck. This allowed us to showcase our business cards, letterhead, and invoices, all with a clear message that highlighted our expertise in providing floor-care systems and solutions.

As our business started to grow rapidly, it became clear that I needed to delegate some of the accounts to other salespeople so that I could focus on pursuing bigger opportunities. This led me to the task of interviewing potential candidates for the job. The process was eye-opening, as most of the applicants were primarily interested in salary, commissions, and expense accounts. It made me wonder whatever happened to the idea of earning your way.

However, I also understood that people needed to make a living, so I devised a plan that included a combination of salary and commission for a set period. This way, the salespeople would have the opportunity to prove themselves and earn their keep.

In the early stages of my business, I encountered some challenges with the work habits and level of determination among my sales team. I remember holding individual meetings with them, informing them that their compensation structure would soon transition to straight commissions. To my surprise, they quickly disappeared, much like the roadrunner. It became evident that I had made poor hiring decisions and failed to find personnel who were the right fit for the job.

Many people advised me to hire individuals from within the industry, assuming they would bring the business knowledge and experience needed. However, my own experience taught me that this approach often resulted in disappointment. Not only did they fail to deliver the promised business, but they also brought along resistance to change, hindering our progress.

I would be interested in conducting a study, if possible, on the turnover rate and expenses associated with salespeople in the cleaning industry. I can only imagine that these figures are astronomical.

Finding the right salespeople is imperative for the success of any business, unless, like me, you prefer to take on all the responsibilities yourself, which only leads to burn out later.

In my quest to find a solution for outsourcing equipment service, I came across a gentleman located in Carmel, a neighboring town to Westfield. It was fortunate timing, as he had just started his own business. Our partnership proved to be mutually beneficial, as we supported each other's growth. We regularly dropped off our equipment at his facility, and he consistently provided prompt turnaround times and exceptional service and repair work.

I established a valuable partnership with a chemical manufacturer based in Canada. Their innovative chemistry offered a unique selling point in my market, allowing us to differentiate ourselves from competitors. Together, we worked diligently to grow our businesses, and their lead share program proved to be highly effective. One lead turned out to be a remarkable account-a nursing home chain in the Midwest that already had a companion company on the East Coast purchasing their floor-care chemicals with excellent results.

To gain a deeper understanding of their standard operating procedures (SOPs), I arranged a meeting with the Midwest company. They had been purchasing a well-known brand but were growing increasingly frustrated with the brand's consistent inability to service their twenty-two locations throughout the state of Indiana.

During our initial meeting, I distinctly remember the owner expressing their priorities. They emphasized that while competitive pricing was important, their focus was on service support and training. They made it clear that if any of their facilities required chemicals or equipment servicing, they expected our company to respond on the same day. The owner looked directly at me and posed the question, "Are you ready for that challenge?"

In response, I assured them that we were prepared to meet their expectations. We offered simplified processes for everything, from ordering based on their established formulary to setting up delivery and training schedules. We also emphasized our commitment to measuring our serviceability. The owner was impressed and made a significant commitment by moving all their business over to us, which amounted to a substantial volume. Additionally, they mentioned that they paid in twenty-five days.

The significance of that account was that it allowed us to establish a strong presence in that city. With this foundation in place, we were able to strategically build additional accounts around them, making it more cost-effective to deliver to rural areas. To further optimize our operations, we carefully scheduled our routes to include stops along the way, thereby reducing the burden of the cost to serve.

We expanded our customer base to include the banking business, hospitals, and educational markets. This diversification played a pivotal role in bringing everything together and solidifying our success.

We provided exceptional service, even during unexpected situations. I would often receive calls late in the evening, around 10:00 p.m., from facilities that had unexpectedly run out of product. Sometimes, their census would increase, requiring them to have product for the next day. In response, I would immediately drive to the warehouse, load up the box truck, and embark on a journey, even if it meant traveling two and a half hours to reach some of these facilities.

Our commitment to delivering on our promises paid off. The owner of the nursing homes was extremely pleased with our service and rewarded us with an additional eleven nursing homes in the state of Arkansas. This presented us with a logistical challenge, but we were determined to fulfill our commitment. I vividly remember loading up the box truck and making the journey to Arkansas to make all eleven deliveries.

To ensure consistent supply, we established a monthly delivery schedule. If they ever ran out of supplies, we would promptly send them via UPS. This approach was crucial in blocking a national distributor from taking over the entire account due to their logistical capabilities.

The International Executive Housekeepers Association (IEHA) chapter meeting presented a valuable opportunity for me to connect with numerous acute care hospitals across the state. During this time, I had the pleasure of meeting Brenda, who was responsible for overseeing a large university, and Sister Martha Ann, who managed three hospitals. Both individuals served on the board of the chapter and eventually became loyal customers of mine.

They were impressed with my innovative suggestions for building membership and revitalizing the chapter. As a result, they encouraged me to run for the position of chapter president. Together, we organized trade shows and engaging activities that fostered unity among members.

However, when it came time for re-election, Franciscan Alliances, Sister Martha Ann, who is known for her competitive nature, decided to challenge me. She even participated in mini-marathons to demonstrate her determination on and off the clock. At that point, my business was growing rapidly, and I found myself lacking the time to fully dedicate to the membership. On election day, Sister had managed to gather support from members I had never even met before. She had stacked the deck in her favor, resulting in her victory.

Despite the unexpected outcome, Sister and I found humor in the situation and shared many laughs. Our friendship has remained strong ever since that day.

A significant rehabilitation center, which was a member of IEHA, eventually became a valuable customer. However, earning their business was not an easy task. Larry, the head of EVS, had a skeptical mindset of "show me" as he hailed from Missouri. To win him over, I remember conducting side-by-side demonstrations with our competitors.

What made our approach unique was that I was the only supplier willing to conduct these demonstrations at night. While my competitors had their manufacturers handle the demos and were comfortably sleeping at home, I took the opportunity to call out the distributor salespeople. This allowed me to gain valuable insights about floors during these late-night demos, as my competitors were missing out while watching the late show.

To secure business with Larry, I focused on showcasing positive outcomes in shorter periods of time. I implemented a time-stamping process, which was something the representatives of competitive manufacturers had never considered. By demonstrating speed and tangible results, I was able to earn Larry's trust and ultimately win his business.

As I arrived one day at the dock with the box truck, Larry happened to be there. He expressed his surprise, saying that he had never seen the owner and president personally delivering the product before. In response, I explained that my other team members were handling deliveries in different parts of the state, I wanted to ensure that he received his product promptly. Larry was taken aback and exclaimed, "But I just ordered it this morning!" It was a moment that left us both impressed and amazed.

The bank that initially provided me with a loan was also experiencing expansion, with more than twenty-five locations spread throughout the state. Interestingly, many of these locations were in the same area as the nursing home chain we were servicing. This presented us with a valuable opportunity to serve both the nursing home chain and the bank, maximizing our efforts and resources.

To optimize our operations, we carefully analyzed various factors such as truck space, product profitability per account, and distance to each customer. This allowed us to determine whether it was worth making the trip and if we were generating sufficient profits. I distinctly recall a few instances where I realized, as Eric was pulling out of the dock, that we had taken on accounts that were not financially viable. Unfortunately, we ended up losing money as soon as he left.

In the distribution business, it is important to consider all the factors associated with the cost to serve. Making informed decisions based on profitability and efficiency is essential for long-term success.

Another large banking company approached us through my connection with a supervisor at the building service contractor, who was a key associate working for that prestigious company with a strong presence in the downtown Class A building sector. He informed me that he had a friend who worked as a facility manager at this finance company, overseeing eleven large buildings on the north side of town. With his help, I was able to arrange a meeting with the facility manager. During the meeting, he provided me with a list of products and challenged me to showcase what we could offer. While he was primarily concerned with price, I saw an opportunity to revamp their delivery systems and reduce their overall budget. To his surprise, I presented a proposal that went beyond just pricing. He exclaimed, "I've never had anyone approach me like this before!" and eagerly asked when we could begin. It wasn't solely about price; it was about finding ways to decrease their overall expenses. I vividly remember personally changing out hundreds of dispensers. As a business owner, I made sure to prioritize getting the job done myself instead of waiting for manufacturers to assist. I couldn't afford to wait, so I took charge of the conversion process.

It was time to hire another driver, and we were fortunate to find a great young man named Danny. He immediately took on the added responsibilities and proved to be a valuable addition to our team. With the addition of another driver, we also acquired another box truck. As a result, I assigned Danny to deliver a specific route while Eric handled deliveries in a different area. Each morning, I met them early to ensure they were properly loaded. Our loading approach was unique and efficient, which many would find impressive. We loaded one side of the truck with pallets from our facility and then stopped by the master distributor early in the morning to pick up an additional six-to-eight pallets. This allowed us to exceed our zero back-order policy, which was highly appreciated by our customers. By eliminating the soft costs of doing business, such as fewer purchase orders and invoices, we were able to simplify our operations and reduce expenses.

My team occasionally complained about having to navigate around pallets to access the products. In response, I asked them if they preferred to go back to the same account with only a few boxes. During lunchtime, I was busy receiving shipments, scheduling future shipments, reviewing incoming orders, and planning the most efficient routes. Eric and Danny returned around noon, and I was prepared to reload their trucks and send them back on the road. Our ability to provide same-day delivery often amazed our customers. If they placed their order before 11:00 a.m., there was a high chance they would receive it that same afternoon. Just imagine being able to order janitorial products and receiving them on the same day. As a small company, we were able to adapt quickly, but it would be much more challenging in today's business landscape. The importance of speed in service cannot be underestimated, especially when considering the impact of B2B trends and the rise of Amazon. I will delve into the effects on the janitorial industry in later chapters of this book.

I remember the impact of the 2008 recession, but despite the challenging economic climate, our business continued to thrive. We were relentless in our pursuit of new opportunities, and time seemed to fly by in a blur. We were incredibly fortunate that the recession didn't hit us as hard as it did others. The only noticeable effect was that our customers started delaying their payments, causing our receivables to stretch out. To address this, I would personally visit the local postal service facility and insist on receiving our mail early. I had developed a reputation for being demanding, but they understood the circumstances and accommodated my request for six months. If checks didn't arrive on time, I immediately contacted the customer and reminded them that while they might be feeling the effects of the recession, it was important not to let both of us suffer. They had received their cleaning products, and we needed to be paid for our services. Throughout the years I ran my company, we only had to write off less than $500 in bad debt. Considering the eight-year span, I believe that was a commendable achievement.

During that period, I actively sought out recession-proof customers, which led me to meet with the owner of a supermarket chain. He expressed dissatisfaction with the condition of his floors, and I assured him that I could improve their appearance at a reduced cost. This was exactly what he needed. Even though people were cutting down on their food expenses, I implemented cost-effective systems that delivered cleaner outcomes. Since the supermarket chain had locations throughout the state, it aligned perfectly with our strategy of filling delivery gaps within our expanding logistics map. This venture marked my first foray into the food retailing industry, and I made sure to document the transformation with plenty of before and after pictures. I strongly recommend that salespeople incorporate this concept into their sales toolbox, as visual evidence is crucial for measuring success.

I have fond memories of receiving numerous awards at the Triple-S Clean Team meetings. Within the association, I was considered an up-and-coming figure. One evening, I had the opportunity to have a quick dinner with John, the executive

VP of the organization. It's remarkable how small our industry can be, as John happened to be the executive mentioned in chapter four when we had to reverse our decision to partner with Grainger. During our conversation, John turned to me and remarked, "You're a lone ranger." He explained that he had never encountered or heard of anyone who had started a business from scratch in our industry and achieved success. I shared with him my simple yet rewarding approach. Before every customer meeting, I made sure to have quotes prepared in advance. My goal was to shorten the sales cycle. Prior to the meetings, I conducted thorough research, which often involved conducting walk-throughs or what is now referred to as site surveys. I aimed to identify the customers' pain points and came prepared with solutions before our official meeting. This practice proved effective for me, as I made the time to thoroughly prepare. As a result, the customers' demeanor changed during the meeting, and I was in control. They recognized that I had done my homework and was genuinely there to make a difference.

Do you remember those suppliers who were skeptical and hesitant to do business with us when we first opened our doors? Well, things changed. We were now purchasing truckloads, and suddenly they came knocking on our door. It was quite satisfying to meet with them and inform them that we had already made commitments to other suppliers who took a chance on our company from the beginning. As our business grew, I began to leverage the back-end rebates, maximizing the benefits and rewards that came with our increased purchasing power.

From the years between 2012-2014, I found myself being pursued by numerous competitors in the market who were interested in acquiring my business. I entertained many of these offers and went through the evaluation process with them. It became evident that my presence in the field was causing them some discomfort. This back-and-forth continued for about six months to a year. However, I remained uninterested in selling unless they could guarantee job security for my employees. That was a nonnegotiable condition for me. Despite my firm stance, I couldn't ignore the toll working sixteen-to-eighteen-hour days was taking on my physical and mental well-being. I began to question whether it was the right time to sell. One thing I knew I wouldn't miss was the backbreaking task of handling and distributing bags of ice melt. While I recognized that I wasn't getting any younger, I still had a deep love for the business we had built. It was a dilemma that many people face at some point in their lives, weighing health and longevity against the continuation of their business.

Mark, who owned a large packaging company, had previously attempted to enter the janitorial business through an acquisition that did not reap the returns expected. This was his second attempt, and I found Mark to be a true gentleman, someone I would be happy to work for if I decided to sell the business and stay on board. I remember meeting with Mark at a bar, enjoying a few drinks, and discussing the agreement. He agreed to the terms, and ultimately, I sold my company to him in 2014.

It was imperative for me to foster open and transparent communication with my employees regarding the sale of the business. I addressed their concerns, provided reassurance, and made sure to maintain morale throughout the entire process. In fact, Mark and his son, Blaine, took the initiative to personally meet with my employees to discuss a smooth transition plan for every employee, offering them an improved package. This gesture meant a great deal to me, as I wanted to ensure that my employees benefited from the acquisition.

I had complete trust in Mark and his family business, as their core principles aligned with mine. My commitment was to make their facilities division the best in the tri-state area, and I was fully dedicated to achieving that goal.

Lessons Learned

- Develop a thorough and creditable business plan.

- It is advisable to make conservative forecasts.

- Identify your specific target market and focus all your energy to achieve success.

- If you are in a business that operates at night or 24/7, it is important not to turn your phone off at 6:00 p.m.

- Seek out opportunities for customers to expand and diversify their businesses.

- Prioritize generating profits for your customers before considering your own gains.

- Discover innovative ways to "WOW" and impress your customers.

- If you decide to sell your business, ensure that you have control over the sale process.

CHAPTER 8

BUILDING A COMPANY
WITHIN A COMPANY

The packaging company that acquired my company, was known for its strong family values. Under the leadership of Mark, the owner, the company implemented a successful "right seat right person" philosophy, ensuring that each employee was in the appropriate role. Mark had a dedicated team of leadership who were instrumental in driving the company's growth. Many of these team members were family members who played a significant role in the company's success, along with an expert in packaging, Eric. Mark's primary goal was to expand the business by offering a comprehensive range of products to complement their core packaging business. This led to the acquisition of my company and the hiring of a highly experienced safety expert, who focused on employee safety compliance. Mark assembled the team of packaging, janitorial, and safety experts to develop strategic plans for customer consolidation and integration. His son, Blaine, who served as the president, was tasked with exploring new opportunities to enhance our sales approach and expand our customer base.

Transitioning from being a business owner for eight years to working for someone else presented its challenges, but surprisingly, I found it easier to adapt than expected. I joined a team of seasoned professionals in the packaging industry, who had previously attempted to expand into janitorial supplies through an acquisition. Unfortunately, the integration did not go as planned, and the existing salesforce they acquired was resistant to change and reluctant to adapt.

In my case, my business setup was slightly different, as I had control over my own account base and a personal drive to retain and grow the business that came with my company. The real challenge lay in winning over the sales team, who had reservations about incorporating janitorial supplies into their existing accounts. It was understandable that they would be hesitant, considering the difficulties they faced during the previous integration, which caused some pain. It was only natural for them to be cautious about jeopardizing their successful packaging business by introducing janitorial products.

Winning over the sales force was not a difficult task, as they recognized my commitment to helping them protect their market share from competitors by leveraging supply chain efficiencies. Additionally, the company made a strategic decision to hire a seasoned professional in the safety business, further emphasizing their dedication to providing comprehensive expertise to customers. This approach added significant value to our offerings, enabling us to explore cross-selling opportunities and approach customers from various angles. We referred to this approach as a "total solution," and it proved to be the right direction for our business. As a result, we were able to expand our presence within existing accounts and unlock new opportunities. By simplifying the business and streamlining the customers' procurement process, we were able to eliminate unnecessary costs and redundancies.

I have a vivid memory of our first sales meeting. The team seemed a bit hesitant, but I had a well-thought-out game plan that they appreciated. We decided to start with the low-hanging fruit, focusing on add-on products that could be easily incorporated into our existing customers. The packaging group was accustomed to handling pallet shipments directly, so we began by targeting higher volume products that could be moved in this manner. It was unexpected for me to start with consumables, but it proved to be the most efficient way to build volume while minimizing the need for extensive service, particularly in floor cleaning. Our primary objective was to establish a presence in the restrooms of large industrial accounts. We initially started with branded products and eventually transitioned to a private brand, which allowed us to protect margins and gain a competitive edge.

The onboarding process for the company was swift and straightforward. We wasted no time and hit the streets almost immediately. My role was to develop the facilities division and collaborate with our branch locations, of which we had three in the Midwest. Additionally, I was tasked with identifying potential strategic acquisitions that could help us enter new markets. If the acquisition began with janitorial supplies, we planned to supplement with packaging salespeople to fully capitalize on the market. Both salesforces would have access to experts who could assist them in addressing key issues and finding effective total solutions.

The company was a proud member of the Afflink association, which consisted of various packaging, janitorial, and food service companies. Over time, the association expanded to include office suppliers as well. I remember numerous meetings where we discussed the integration of janitorial supplies with members who were interested in adding this category to their overall product offerings. During these discussions, I emphasized that there are two distinct approaches to integration.

The first approach involves targeting high-volume, medium to low-profit business opportunities. This typically entails focusing on restroom supplies in industrial plants, as most administrative areas are often outsourced to cleaning contractors. However, these contractors can serve as excellent future customers, as they are responsible for cleaning numerous industrial buildings and have valuable contacts.

The second approach is more technical and service-oriented, specifically addressing the cleaning needs of the plant floor. This involves providing chemicals and equipment to maintain clean and safe floors. Finding experts in this field or relying on manufacturers can sometimes be challenging. However, since the flooring composition primarily consists of concrete and the restrooms feature ceramic with grout, I found it relatively straightforward to develop programs that effectively addressed their cleaning challenges. When selling floor-care systems to industrial accounts, simplicity and reliability are key, as the equipment must withstand the daily wear and tear of the industrial environment. Through my involvement in membership meetings, I had the opportunity to meet some remarkable individuals who would play a significant role in future endeavors.

I was captivated by a packaging presentation I attended one day, which sparked my interest in the industry. Subsequently,

I enrolled in a comprehensive training course led by a third-party packaging industry consultant. As I delved deeper into the training exercises, I began to realize that providing solutions is a daily occurrence in this supply category. It involves finding ways to save customers money through more scientific and efficient methods. This approach aligned perfectly with my expertise in solution selling.

Additionally, I discovered that selling packaging was comparatively easier because it encompassed a wide range of areas that required preparation and expertise. On the other hand, janitorial supplies involve numerous SKUs and often require delivering smaller quantities, which can be costlier for the company. It surprises me that there aren't more janitorial companies venturing into the packaging industry. With many individuals aging out of the janitorial and packaging industries, I believe the main challenge lies in finding qualified salespeople who are willing to work, sell, and remain committed to the trade.

Prioritizing our focus on consumables, I recognized the need to develop a tool that we referred to as the "savings snapshot." This digital spreadsheet was designed to provide a clear comparison between the customer's existing products and our own offerings. On one side of the spreadsheet, we listed the customer's current products, while on the adjacent side, we presented our own products or comparable alternatives. The spreadsheet guided us towards the middle where we input our price per unit. The customer then input their price per unit and unit of measure, ensuring an apples-to-apples comparison. This also provided them with a quick and detailed annualized volume and unit price comparative.

To enhance usability, we categorized the snapshot, grouping all paper products in one zone, soaps in another, and so on. This allowed the customer to quickly assess their supply spend on product categories and determine the potential savings in each category, as well as the overall savings they could achieve by incorporating these products into their existing supply spend. The savings snapshot provided reliable data for the customer to make an informed decision to convert.

I also saw the need to develop a supply chain calculator that helped highlight the soft savings in operational and administrative areas. This tool made it easier for our sales team to promote add-on products, while also enabling the customer to reduce both hard and soft costs.

During my tenure, one of my top priorities was to establish a rep council that would assist us in developing effective sales programs across all divisions of the company. This council, known as a "crossover event," aimed to simplify the business for nonfacilities representatives, ensuring they were well-informed and motivated to sell the total solution. The primary objective was to leverage the strengths and address the weaknesses.

The council meetings focused on key aspects of the business, including supplier selections, supplier consolidation, customer retention strategies, target accounts, our private label program, year-over-year comparisons, statistical point systems, seasonal products, vendor and vertical sales training, upselling techniques, value-based selling, software training and utilization, service programs, and delivery and logistics.

The purpose of establishing this council was twofold: to foster team unity and to gather valuable insights and direction from the field. By involving representatives, we aimed to shape the facilities division for years to come, ensuring its continued success and growth.

Upselling and selling value were key components of our division's success. To effectively implement these strategies, we first needed to identify the main requirements for selling value and quantify its monetary worth. This led us to develop a project called the Value Calculator. Through this calculator, we were able to demonstrate to customers the savings and value we provided on a quarterly basis. These values were categorized into five key areas: procurement, possession, application, materials, and labor.

The Value Calculator was supported by various initiatives and drivers, including supply chain reduction analysis, comprehensive cost reduction analysis, inventory management and assessment systems, site surveys, customized training programs, total quality management training, industry workbooks, training on each segment of cleaning, customized SDS books, system cleaning analysis, material cost reduction plans, product usage reports, cleaning reduction plans, labor reduction analysis, work loading, and visualization of the level of cleanliness. These initiatives played a pivotal role in differentiating our company from competitors who solely focused on pricing products. By offering a wide range of value-added services, it became difficult for clients to overlook the benefits they received at no additional cost. This approach fostered team unity with our customers and eliminated the need to solely compete on price.

One area where we truly stood out from the competition was in conducting site surveys. When customers agreed to a site survey, we took the opportunity to differentiate ourselves by thoroughly assessing their facility and gathering essential information. During these surveys, we would walk through the facility and engage in meaningful conversations to build a comprehensive plan.

The site surveys were structured to cover key areas, including customer information, facility details, labor efficiencies, sustainability practices, training and education needs, safety compliance, distribution services, and product sections categorized by different areas of the facility. This encompassed chemicals, consumables, and equipment.

The time we invested in learning about the customers' business and understanding their specific needs proved to be incredibly valuable. Based on the findings from the site survey, we would then construct a tailored plan that aimed to deliver cleaner outcomes while reducing costs. Additionally, we provided value-added services that aligned with their facility requirements. By taking this comprehensive approach, we were able to demonstrate our commitment to meeting their unique needs and delivering exceptional results.

In addition, we developed a market-specific calculator that was tailored to different industries, including manufacturing, building service contractors, education, food processing, warehousing, and healthcare. This calculator proved to be a valuable tool for our sales team as it allowed them to effectively assess key factors related to each customer. These factors included the type of customer, number of employees, level of decision-making authority, identification of door openers, and selection of key innovations. The calculator also consisted of twelve leading questions that corresponded to twelve specific responses. AI possibilities for the future. By utilizing this calculator, our sales team could accurately determine the value that each customer was seeking. Furthermore, it provided our salespeople with the necessary information to address customer inquiries and develop customized plans that exceeded their expectations.

This approach allowed us to truly understand and address the unique needs of each customer.

The facilities division had a strong focus on building service contractors. During this time, I developed various industry return-on-investment calculators that helped determine the number of full-time employees required for a job, budgetary support for proposal preparation, and materials needed for procurement based on standard operating procedures outlined in the request for proposal. These calculators provided contractors with a comprehensive approach to securing jobs. I remember working with a gentleman named Lewis who was just starting his company. Together, we successfully won several significant contracts that propelled his company to become a leading contender in the marketplace. Our professional relationship has remained strong, and I continue to assist him as an advisor to his company. This serves as a prime example of how adding value to a business relationship can result in mutual success.

We strongly believed in the importance of training our customers, which led us to develop a comprehensive monthly training program. We invited customers from various markets to participate in these sessions. The topics covered in these training programs were diverse and aimed to address specific industry needs. Some of the topics included healthcare benchmarking, guidance on selecting the appropriate building service contractor, preparing standard operating procedures in food processing, matching floor types to cleaning processes, implementing employee recognition programs, streamlining supply chain consolidation, designing internal preventive maintenance programs, creating effective internal cleaning training programs, optimizing restroom maintenance systems, and establishing a level of clean program in collaboration with customer management. By offering these training programs, we aimed to empower our customers with the knowledge and skills necessary to excel in their respective industries.

Mark and Blaine were firm believers in the importance of structure, which led them to seek assistance from the entrepreneurial operating system (EOS). This system, known for its effectiveness, offered clear visual representations of the six crucial elements that businesses need to effectively manage to achieve success: vision, data, process, traction, issues, and people. This was my initial exposure to this operating system, and it proved to be invaluable in keeping us focused and accountable. The knowledge I gained from this early experience with EOS would prove to be extremely useful as I progressed throughout my career.

I was sitting in my office one day looking over notes from our L10 meeting when I received a call from Charlie; I noticed that he seemed depressed. It was clear that he wasn't feeling well, and that old age was making it increasingly difficult for him to get around. I reached out to Paul and suggested organizing a reunion so that everyone could express their appreciation for Charlie. We quickly got to work planning the event and decided on a four-day gathering at the Innisbrook Golf Resort, which was conveniently located near Charlie's home. I vividly remember a moment at the bar when I stood next to Carv, our marketing manager, and we momentarily didn't recognize each other because I had grown a beard; after all, it was over twenty-five years since we'd seen one another. The reunion was a success, with over thirty sales reps, office personnel, and administrative staff attending to honor Charlie. The old camaraderie and magic of the past came alive once again. Charlie knew that his sales lieutenants were there to pay their respects one final time, acknowledging the significant impact he had had on their lives. As we bid farewell, we all realized that it would be the last time we would see Charlie.

Charlie was always intrigued about how I'd built the business and sold it. He always wondered about the integration into the packaging world, and I assured him that it was a great Midwest company that already had three branch locations. I had various opportunities to grow my company within their company organically as well as acquiring other companies. Utilizing my knowledge of distributors in the Midwest, I reached out to several potential sellers. One company in Fort Wayne caught our interest as it would grant us access to the northeast region, including Toledo. Another company in Dayton provided access to the Cincinnati and Columbus markets. With the goal of integrating packaging and safety into our offerings, Mark and Blaine successfully acquired both companies. However, these acquisitions brought forth challenges such as navigating cultural differences, aligning compensation plans, integrating systems, retaining customers, and transitioning to a mission of selling a complete bundle encompassing facilities, packaging, and safety.

I remember encountering challenges with the Dayton branch, as we struggled to find the right manager to lead and develop that location. To address these issues, I volunteered to step in and help grow that market. My initial focus was on evaluating the salesforce. Additionally, I conducted a thorough assessment of the branch's strengths and weaknesses. Fortunately, we had several representatives who successfully transitioned into selling packaging, which proved to be a positive development.

Another area of focus was customer retention and expanding our presence within existing accounts. To achieve this, I collaborated with the sales team to organize several events. The first event was a customer recognition outing at the Dayton Dragons, where we secured a prime location on the right field with food and drinks. This allowed us to personally connect with our customers and build stronger relationships both on a personal and business level, all while enjoying the game. It turned out to be a memorable and enjoyable night for everyone involved. You tend to overestimate attendance. Customers sign up, but sometimes unforeseen circumstances prevent them from attending. Despite having a good turnout, I remember having leftover catered food. I informed Mark and Blaine that I would personally visit some homeless shelters and donate the leftovers, which was a very rewarding experience.

The second event was a customer appreciation golf outing, which exceeded my expectations. Working closely with one of our dedicated sales representatives, Camila, we successfully organized an outing that attracted over one hundred customers. To make the day even more special, we incorporated an awards ceremony that recognized our valued suppliers. The event was a resounding success, with attendees already inquiring about the plans for next year. It became evident that building personal connections with customers went beyond mere business associations. Additionally, we had the support of our suppliers who sponsored the event. Throughout my career, I have attended numerous golf outings, but none of them matched the level of dedication and attention to detail that we achieved that afternoon.

During our team calls with customers, there were instances where the dynamic could be a bit overwhelming, as three highly trained and experienced professionals vied for time to present their respective offerings. However, amidst the intensity, I formed a close friendship with Kent, the safety expert. We discovered that we shared similar paths in our lives, both having started companies from the ground up and eventually selling them. Our camaraderie led to many lighthearted moments where we would sit and laugh for hours. While we all had a strong desire to shine in our respective areas of expertise, we also recognized that we were just a small component within the larger packaging side of the business, which had experienced significant growth over the years. Nevertheless, we were making valuable contributions by introducing a new dimension to the company.

One realization that the packaging salespeople had was the emergence of janitorial companies venturing into the packaging market. To prevent overexposure and maintain our customer base, it was important for us to block any attempts by these competitors to infiltrate our customers. On the other hand, selling safety products was saving lives, as industrial-based accounts placed a high emphasis on safety standards. I truly miss selling alongside Kent, especially our post-call debriefing sessions. These debriefings often revealed humorous aspects of our meetings and proved to be just as valuable, if not more, than the meetings themselves. Most importantly, we had fun while selling. As a motivational ritual before heading out to make sales calls, we would play Japanese war drums, setting a positive and energetic tone that carried into our meetings and ultimately helped us win over customers.

The principle of placing the right person in the right seat is particularly critical in the context of wholesale distribution. Salespeople possess unique strengths and weaknesses, and I developed a team selling concept that aimed to leverage these strengths to create a powerful and unified team. The concept was relatively simple: visualizing the compensation pool and identifying a representative, known as the opener, as the basis for the pool. Their income, typically commission-based, would be considered. Additionally, the maintainer, responsible for lead generation and account maintenance, would contribute their earnings, which could be a combination of salary and commissions. The customer service representative's compensation, usually salary-based, and the technology support personnel's compensation would also be added to the team compensation.

Once the individual team members' earnings were established, it became apparent that the opener would need to sacrifice a portion of their earnings to gain the full backing and support of the team. They would benefit by opening more new businesses and their time would be dedicated to closing opportunities. The objective was to position everyone in a way that allowed them to contribute their strengths and time commitment to business growth. Although this structure was never implemented, it was discussed among the leadership team. I firmly believe that in wholesale distribution, this type of structure could serve as a differentiating factor, effectively addressing the challenges associated with pursuing and retaining new business.

One accomplishment that truly stood out among others was the development of our private label program. It took companies greater than ten years to build a comprehensive private label program, and we did in it in eighteen months We carefully selected the best products in each cleaning segment to be incorporated into this program. While the program achieved a level of success, it didn't quite meet my personal standards for success. Selling a private label is inherently more challenging than selling a well-known brand. However, once we sold the program within an account, it became incredibly difficult for competitors to displace us. While it may have been harder to sell, it also proved to be harder to remove once implemented. I am confident the program continued to thrive and meet the standards of success.

As I reflected on my past and contemplated the future, I felt a strong desire to leverage my experience to assist other companies in achieving success. This realization prompted me to seriously consider establishing a consulting business, as I believed it was the right time to embark on the next phase of my professional journey. With my extensive experience in acquiring and selling businesses, I knew I had valuable insights to offer an industry on the brink of significant consolidation.

Lessons Learned

- Ensuring that the right person is in the right seat within a company can help prevent unfair expectations arising between individuals.

- Seek a total solution supported by industry experts that includes educating, training, and sales support in closing deals.

- Be willing to invest time in learning and selling tangible products that may be outside of your comfort zone.

- Make it convenient for your customers to compare your products and prices at their own convenience. Speed up the sales cycle.

- By identifying the soft costs and validating the savings, you can assess the financial and operational benefits of standardization and consolidation.

- Before providing value, monetize it for your customers, or be taken for granted.

- Create a positive environment where your customers are motivated to help you succeed.

- Making your customer appreciation day memorable creates a unique and enjoyable experience that reflects your appreciation.

CHAPTER 9

MERGERS AND ACQUISITIONS

D etermined to find my next challenge, I considered consulting. I thought I could offer a diverse portfolio of services. My extensive experience in distribution and manufacturing could benefit pulling together a community that had been divided for some time. The one area that intrigued me the most was the mergers and acquisitions (M and A) area. Remember the predictions in Chapter 5 based on that industry study? Those disruptions were now happening at a rapid pace. I will share some of my experiences and provide suggestions for those considering buying or selling companies.

Acquiring companies in the distribution and manufacturing sectors, I have observed that while these industries differ significantly, the process of evaluating a company's value remains largely similar. When it comes to purchasing distribution businesses, my approach ranged from a quick initial assessment to a more systematic and thorough analysis.

Acquiring Distribution Companies

The initial quick view I learned from Ames involved a straightforward assessment process where we aligned our initial evaluation with the market value. During an initial meeting with the company's ownership, we gathered information regarding their operations, such as revenue, employee count (particularly in the warehouse), number of trucks, ownership status of the building, existing suppliers, and any affiliations with industry associations. Based on this information, we employed a simple scale to determine the company's worth. If the company met our criteria and was well-managed, we would consider acquiring it at a cost equivalent to 50 percent of its revenues. If it fell slightly short but possessed key components, we would consider a purchase of 40 percent of revenues. For mediocre companies, we would consider a purchase at 30 percent of revenues. Any company that did not meet these three levels did not pique our interest in further financial negotiations. It was during the subsequent financial analysis that we gained true visibility into how the owner operated the company. In most cases, our quick view assessment proved to be fairly accurate. It helped us prioritize companies that were a good fit for our acquisition strategy, while also identifying those that would require significant time and effort to integrate into our system or had a longer return on investment timeline that didn't align with our goals. This approach allowed us to focus our resources on opportunities that had the potential for a more favorable outcome.

We found that some companies at the 30 percent level presented good buying opportunities, as we believed we could quickly elevate them to meet our standards and acquire them at a favorable price. These were typically referred to as turnaround opportunities in the M & A industry. On the other hand, companies that fell below our scale were deemed too demanding and distracting to consider, regardless of the sale price.

Once we identified a company that fit within our scale, we expressed interest in proceeding to the next round of negotiations. This involved conducting a comprehensive evaluation process, where we focused on specific areas when acquiring distribution businesses.

During our evaluation process, we thoroughly examined the company's financial statements, paying close attention to key factors such as revenue, profitability, cash flow, and debt levels. Our focus was particularly centered on margins, as they provided valuable insights into the company's culture and core principles. With our significant buying volume, we often identified opportunities to increase gross margins by 2-4 percent, depending on the company's size. Additionally, we considered the impact of our volume addition on supplier rebates, which served as an advantage for us. We also assessed the current suppliers and evaluated the potential for transitioning to our own suppliers, as this could further enhance margins. Overall, the standard financial review helped us gauge whether our initial assessment using the quick view aligned with the company's actual financial performance.

We ensured that our offer was based on a fair multiple of earnings before taxes and amortization (EBTA). In most cases, our evaluation was quite accurate. However, if there were factors that we believed would be beneficial in the negotiation process, we would consider offering at our cost an evaluation of the company by a third party. This approach helped us maintain transparency and fairness throughout the acquisition process.

During our assessment, we thoroughly evaluated the company's competitive advantage, market share, and industry trends. We also took into consideration factors such as the company's reputation, customer base, and potential for future growth. Obtaining this information was relatively straightforward through the reporting they provided.

One area we particularly focused on was the customer base and any overlap with our existing customers. When acquiring a distribution company to expand into a new market, the potential gain is significant, often reaching 100 percent. However, it is crucial to consider customer retention, an aspect that many buying companies tend to overlook during their research.

On the other hand, when acquiring a company in our own backyard, we conducted a thorough analysis of cross-pollination of accounts. This involved examining which salesperson would manage the account, as it posed a dilemma. In most cases, the decision was based on the salesperson with the stronger relationship and sales performance, as these factors often go hand in hand.

Assessing the experience, expertise, and track record of the management team often occurs after the sale, as they are typically not involved in the negotiation process unless they have ownership stakes. However, we gathered input from the owner regarding the management team. Since the owner's involvement was limited after the sale, we identified potential candidates for branch manager positions to fill the leadership gap. In some cases, we established a time limit for the owner to assist with the transition.

It was imperative for us to identify a strong leadership team capable of driving the company's growth and effectively navigating challenges. However, due to our nondisclosure agreement (NDA), we had to be cautious in seeking information about the management team from industry personnel or relying on the owner's word. Maintaining confidentiality was a priority throughout the evaluation process.

In evaluating the company's growth prospects, we examined both organic growth potential and the possibility of acquisitions. Specifically, we explored the concept of cluster acquisitions, where we assessed whether there were other complementary companies in the same area as the target company. This analysis involved considering the potential benefits of consolidating warehouses, personnel, and leveraging the customer base, particularly if the markets served were different. We conducted a quick review to determine if such a strategy made sense and if there were viable options to consider.

Additionally, we considered factors such as market demand, potential for product or service innovation, and expansion opportunities. When assessing growth, we also evaluated the company's sales force, often following the 80-20 rule. This rule suggests that 80 percent of the business is typically generated by 20 percent of the salesforce. Understanding the effectiveness and performance of the sales team was crucial in evaluating growth potential.

It is essential to thoroughly examine the current compensation plan for your sales team when considering an acquisition. Specifically, we focused on the 20 percent of salespeople who were considered hunters and assessed whether they would benefit from our acquisition of the company. Retaining 80 percent of the business was a key factor for us. The remaining 20 percent typically consisted of maintainers or inside accounts. We assessed the maintainers to identify individuals with the potential to transition into professional salespeople. Subsequently, we introduced a training program aimed at equipping these maintainers with the skills and mindset required to become successful hunters. This strategic investment yielded significant returns, particularly when we discovered a few exceptional talents among them.

In 1995, we had the opportunity to make a significant acquisition. The company we were considering was located within a forty-mile radius of our warehouse and had a customer base that would have provided us access to 75 percent of new customers. It was critical for us to retain the sales representatives who had a significant influence on that business. As the acquisition was nearing completion, we encountered some challenges. Unfortunately, I had a prior commitment out of the country and could not be present during the final stages. This led to a few holdouts among the sales representatives. I was concerned that they might take their business elsewhere or secure funding from another company to start a competing venture. Unfortunately, this scenario unfolded, and we lost a portion of that business. However, some customers who were more loyal to the products than to the sales representatives remained with us. Although the impact was not significant, we did open the door to competition by not securing all the sales representatives. It is important to remember that in this industry, people buy from people, and building strong relationships with customers can provide security.

After that lesson and to protect our interests, we tied the salespeople's noncompete agreement to the sale of the company. It was imperative for us that everyone transitioned to our company; otherwise, the deal would not proceed. This practice proved to be highly effective, as it motivated the owner to ensure the successful transition. In some cases, we even provided incentives to the owner to facilitate this process.

Customer retention was an important aspect that demanded a thorough examination from multiple perspectives. Recognizing that in the janitorial supply industry approximately 15 percent of business is nonrepetitive, we dedicated a section of the sale process to focus on customer retention. To evaluate this, we considered the percentage of retention over a three-year period, and if the numbers did not meet the expected benchmarks, the payout was adjusted accordingly. This approach allowed us to identify any contracts or significant business segments that might have been at risk. Additionally, we considered factors such as the relationships between sales representatives and customers, the acceptance of current products, potential changes, and existing service requirements. Considering all these factors enabled us to assess the potential for retaining customers and ensured a smooth transition. Once the acquisition was announced, we recognized that timing was critical and promptly established a comprehensive schedule for personally visiting the high-producing customers within the initial week.

During the legal and regulatory compliance review, our objective was to ensure that the company adhered to all relevant laws and regulations. This process involved identifying any potential legal or regulatory risks that could potentially affect the acquisition.

In terms of customer and supplier relationships, we sought to gain a comprehensive understanding of the company's customer base, customer loyalty, and the nature of their relationships with key suppliers. We evaluated the strength of these relationships and assessed their potential impact on future business prospects.

However, it is important to note that obtaining an accurate read on these customer and supplier relationships during the due diligence phase could be challenging due to the nondisclosure agreement (NDA) in place. The NDA limited the information we could access and made it difficult to fully assess the dynamics of customer and supplier relationships.

In assessing the company's operational processes, efficiency, and scalability, our focus was on identifying opportunities for streamlining operations, reducing costs, and enhancing output. This is where a thorough review of overall inventory, slow moving, and obsolete inventory play an important factor. Companies that do not properly account for obsolete inventory are generally stuck with nonmoving products that need to be heavily discounted, donated, or thrown away. We also considered whether the acquisition involved any physical locations, such as brick and mortar stores, and evaluated factors such as existing leases. We explored the possibility of assuming leases or relocating to more efficient facilities, potentially enabling us to implement cross-docking strategies if proximity allowed.

In 1996, we embarked on a smaller acquisition that posed several challenges. However, upon conducting a thorough evaluation, we uncovered a significant issue; more than 38 percent of the target company's products were either obsolete or incompatible with the current market demands. This discovery necessitated a revision of our offer, excluding these products from the deal. Unfortunately, this led to disagreements regarding the valuation of the remaining inventory, ultimately resulting in our difficult decision to withdraw from the acquisition. Although disappointing, this experience served as a valuable lesson, emphasizing the critical importance of meticulously assessing a company's product viability and compatibility prior to pursuing an acquisition.

We also carefully evaluated any ongoing litigation and its potential impact on the acquisition. If feasible, we developed strategies to mitigate these risks. However, if the risks were deemed too significant or unmanageable, we opted to exit the process of acquiring the company. Ensuring a thorough assessment of potential legal liabilities was important in making informed decisions during the acquisition process.

Cultural compatibility is often an area that is overlooked but holds significant importance. It involves assessing whether the values, work culture, and management styles of the acquiring and target companies align to facilitate a seamless integration process.

Acquiring Manufacturing Companies

In my experiences of acquiring manufacturing businesses, I have encountered various approaches, ranging from an initial assessment to a more thorough financial evaluation. The initial assessment allows for a preliminary sizing up of the company, while a financial approach involves a more comprehensive analysis.

Regardless of the approach taken, cultural compatibility is the key factor ensuring successful integration and harmonious collaboration between the acquiring and target companies.

Acquiring companies in the manufacturing sector can vary significantly, with the analysis primarily focused on operational efficiency, facility integration, and personnel retainment. When considering a potential acquisition, there are several key operational components to evaluate.

Firstly, it is important to assess whether the products produced by the potential acquisition align with your current product lineup. This consideration is particularly relevant as some manufacturers may also import products. It is imperative to evaluate how existing relationships would transfer or hold up with a new partner.

Additionally, it is essential to determine if the potential acquisition has manufacturing capabilities that complement your own operations logistically. Assessing whether they possess equipment that could enhance cost efficiency, increase production volume, or eliminate the need for outsourcing certain components is also important.

Another factor to consider is the company's movability and whether there are any obstacles to consolidating factories. Evaluating the status and lifespan of any patents on their products is crucial, as well as determining the percentage of the business that relies on these patented products.

By thoroughly examining these operational components, you can gain a comprehensive understanding of the potential acquisition's fit within your manufacturing operations and make informed decisions regarding the acquisition.

In 2000, I received a call from our representative agency in California informing me that a propane manufacturing company was facing financial difficulties and needed to sell the business. I immediately contacted Mike, the owner, and learned that he was dealing with an employee embezzlement issue and was uncertain about the company's future. I promptly enlisted the help of Tom, our vice president of M&A from our parent company, and together we flew out to meet with Mike. The situation was dire-a long-time loyal employee had illicitly obtained all the accounting and banking information and had disappeared without a trace. We diligently examined documents to reconstruct the company's receivables, providing us with an understanding of the outstanding amount of what was owed. We also assessed the company's relationships with suppliers and restructured their payables. It was an intensive day-long effort, but we managed to formulate a fair and equitable offer, including an employment offer for Mike. He proved to be an asset to our company, particularly with his patented design for the Center Fire machine, and vast knowledge of that segment, which was instrumental in growing our business.

When evaluating a potential acquisition, it is essential to assess the revenue-generating aspects, particularly in terms of accessing new distribution channels and exploring opportunities for synergy between the businesses. It is important to evaluate whether the target company has a sales force that can be integrated into your own operations. Alternatively, selecting the top-performing sales candidates from the target company to enhance and restructure your overall sales department can also be beneficial. Evaluating the existing territories and analyzing true market penetration can be relatively straightforward. I recommend utilizing an industry-standard per head assessment to efficiently evaluate salespeople and make informed decisions.

Before showing any interest in acquiring a manufacturing company, we always conducted a quick assessment to address key considerations. This initial evaluation helped us determine if the potential acquisition aligned with our strategic goals and if it was worth further exploration. By conducting this preliminary assessment, we could efficiently filter out unsuitable opportunities and focus on those that had the potential for a successful acquisition.

Once we established that a company had the potential for scalability, we proceeded to the next round of negotiations, conducting a comprehensive evaluation process. When considering the acquisition of a manufacturing company, we focused on several key areas.

One imperative aspect was evaluating the company's financial statements and balance sheets, which included analyzing revenue, profitability, cash flow, inventory and debt levels. We sought consistent growth, healthy profit margins, and a strong balance sheet as indicators of financial stability and potential for future success.

Through a comprehensive evaluation of these financial factors, we obtained valuable insights into the company's overall financial well-being and its capacity to generate consistent profits. Our assessment involved examining obsolete equipment and parts inventory as well as SG&A expense to determine if the company's operations were managed properly or was if there was overspending. Additionally, we analyzed material costs as a percentage of net sales to assess their purchasing practices and to identify potential volume consolidation benefits for us. Furthermore, we scrutinized overhead expenses to ensure appropriate staffing levels.

In 1997, there was a memorable acquisition incident that I heard about from a reliable source. The details of the event were quite amusing yet concerning. During a tour of the manufacturing site, the potential buyer accidentally leaned on a box in the finished goods area, causing them to fall through several boxes that were labeled as finished goods. However, it turned out that the boxes were empty, raising ethical concerns about the company's practices. As a result, the buyers immediately decided to terminate the acquisition and could no longer trust any further negotiations with the seller.

By thoroughly examining all aspects of the business, it usually played a pivotal role in determining the feasibility and desirability of the acquisition opportunity. Assessing these financial indicators, we were able to gauge the company's financial stability, identify areas for potential improvement, and make informed decisions regarding the acquisition.

In addition to evaluating the financial aspects, we also assessed the company's competitive advantage, market share, and industry trends. We considered factors such as the company's reputation, customer base, and potential for future growth. Fortunately, obtaining this information was relatively easier on the manufacturing side as it was readily available.

We placed significant importance on understanding the customer base and their acceptance or willingness to explore complementary products from both companies. This analysis helped us identify opportunities to expand within existing relationships and leverage synergies.

Furthermore, we examined any national, government, or contractual agreements that the company possessed. These agreements presented potential avenues for generating additional revenue and expanding the business.

By thoroughly evaluating these aspects, we gained a comprehensive understanding of the company's competitive position, market potential, and growth opportunities. This information was key in determining the overall attractiveness and potential success of the acquisition.

Assessing the experience, expertise, and track record of the management team was often done after the sale, as it provided a clearer view of their ownership and management style, which was more openly recognized in the industry. We prioritized finding a strong leadership team that could seamlessly integrate into our culture and uphold our core principles. In the past, relocation concerns were more prevalent, but with the rise of remote work, this issue has become less critical, depending on the specific position.

Additionally, we analyzed the company's growth prospects, both organically and through potential acquisitions. Our focus was on determining whether the addition of the company would provide the necessary integration and generate revenues that could lead to a quicker return on investment. This evaluation helped us gauge the potential for future success and aligned with our strategic goals.

The legal and regulatory compliance review was conducted to ensure that the company adhered to all relevant laws and regulations. During this process, we also identified any potential legal or regulatory risks that could potentially impact the acquisition.

In terms of customer and supplier relationships, our focus was on understanding the company's customer base, customer loyalty, and the nature of their relationships with key suppliers. We carefully evaluated the strength of these relationships and assessed their potential impact on future business prospects. It is important to note that obtaining an accurate read on these relationships during the due diligence phase could be challenging due to the nondisclosure agreement in place. However, compared to a distribution acquisition, we were able to gain a clearer vision of the customer and supplier relationships.

By conducting a thorough evaluation of legal compliance and customer/supplier relationships, we aimed to mitigate risks and make informed decisions regarding the acquisition.

We also thoroughly assessed the company's operational processes, efficiency, and scalability. Our focus was on identifying opportunities to streamline operations, reduce costs, and enhance output. In the case of a manufacturing acquisition, the factory and its value were of critical importance. We carefully considered how it fit logistically and its production capabilities. For instance, if you were an East Coast or Midwest manufacturer, the freight expenses and time to serve customers on the West Coast were factors to consider in terms of quicker response to customer needs.

Furthermore, we evaluated the potential impact of any litigation on the acquisition. It was crucial to develop strategies to mitigate these risks and to ensure a smooth transition. Additionally, any regulatory issues raised a red flag and heavily influenced our decision-making process. Compliance with regulations was a key consideration in assessing the viability and potential success of the acquisition.

Cultural compatibility is imperative, yet an often-overlooked aspect in any industry. It encompasses the alignment of values, work culture, and management styles, which are essential for ensuring a seamless integration process. Recognizing the significance of cultural compatibility is vital, regardless of the specific industry involved. By prioritizing this aspect, organizations can foster a harmonious and productive environment during the integration process, leading to greater overall success.

My experiences in acquiring both distribution and manufacturing companies came in handy, and it was time for me to apply that knowledge as I prepared to sell my own business.

Selling a Business

Four competitors expressed interest in acquiring my company, each with varying degrees of interest. As a seller, I had to carefully consider the needs of the potential buyers. Some buyers were primarily interested in acquiring our customer base and eliminating our presence in the marketplace, as we were seen as disruptive. It was evident that these buyers were looking for a bargain and would not be suitable for handing off what we had built.

On the other hand, there were buyers who recognized the value of entering the janitorial supplies industry and were willing to offer a good price for our company. Eventually, we found a buyer who aligned with our vision and goals.

In the final six months leading up to the sale of my company, we engaged in discussions with accountants and potential buyers to explore various possibilities. I found myself in a unique position as I had been responsible for all aspects of the business, meaning that the buyer was essentially acquiring my talent and the ability to replicate what I had built. During meetings with some of the potential buyers, it became apparent that they believed they had everything figured out. However, it is ironic that today, several of those buyers have either sold or had minimal impact on the market.

Sitting on the other side of the acquisition table provided me with valuable insights as I listened to their pitches on how the acquisition would benefit both companies. My primary concern was ensuring that my employees would be retained by the acquiring company. Interestingly, only one buyer explicitly indicated their intention to retain the employees even before I made it a stipulation. This gesture signaled to me that they could potentially be the most suitable suitor for the acquisition.

Many sellers tend to overvalue their companies, but I approached the pricing of my business based on my experience in acquiring other companies. However, the valuation ultimately depends on the unique circumstances surrounding the sale. In my case, I decided to sell because Brenda was concerned about the toll it was taking on my health, and I did not have any family members interested in taking over the business.

Throughout the selling process, I made several observations. I determined the fair market value of my business by carefully considering factors such as financial performance, assets, intellectual property, customer base, and growth potential. I was specifically seeking a buyer who wanted me to contribute to building their own business, rather than simply acquiring me to eliminate a competitor. This aspect played a key role in my decision-making process when selecting the most suitable suitor for the acquisition.

Before proceeding with the sale, it was crucial for me to ensure that my business was in optimal condition. This involved organizing financial records and addressing any operational inefficiencies. Additionally, I considered the timing of the potential sale in relation to my lease agreement for the warehouse space. I recognized that all the assets, including trucks, racking, service tools, office furniture, computers, and more, would be consolidated into the buyer's facility.

Maintaining strict confidentiality throughout the selling process was of utmost importance to safeguard my business's reputation, employee morale, and customer relationships. To achieve this, we implemented nondisclosure agreements (NDAs) when sharing sensitive information.

I developed a comprehensive marketing strategy aimed at attracting potential buyers, highlighting the seamless integration, customer retention, and growth opportunities that our business could offer if acquired.

During the due diligence process, I meticulously prepared detailed information about our business. This included providing financial statements, contracts, employee details, customer data, and any other relevant documentation to facilitate a thorough evaluation by potential buyers.

The negotiation phase with potential buyers primarily focused on key aspects such as the purchase price, payment terms, noncompete agreements, and any contingencies. Approximately six months before the actual sale, our accountants received an offer that fell short of our expectations. In response, I made the decision to hold off on accepting the offer. It was imperative to create a sense of desirability, making them want my company more than I wanted to sell. This waiting game will pay off. If the buyer truly values your company, they will eventually come back with a more favorable offer.

I diligently worked on preparing a transition plan to ensure a seamless handover of the business. If I were to continue working with the new buyer, it was important to invest time in developing this plan. It involved creating a business plan that outlined potential growth opportunities and that would be achieved within the new business environment.

When I finally sold my business, it was important for me to foster open and transparent communication with my employees regarding the sale of the business. I addressed their concerns, provided reassurance, and made sure to maintain morale throughout the entire process. It was mandatory that they all had jobs with the new company before the sale.

Lessons Learned

- You are not just acquiring the business, but rather, you are acquiring the talented individuals who make it successful.

- Assessing inventories is crucial for maximizing your return on investment.

- Building strong relationships with sales representatives should be a top priority of any company, as people tend to buy from people that they trust. Therefore, retaining sales representatives should be a key focus.

- Are you acquiring the business solely to eliminate a competitor, or are you aiming to build upon their achievements? Which type of buyer do you identify as?

- Don't be too quick to sell. If your company holds value, potential buyers will most likely return. Have you ever desired something that was initially out of reach?

- Collaborating through an acquisition and maintaining full transparency can lead to a mutually beneficial outcome.

CHAPTER 10

CONSULTING

I began working part-time in the evenings, offering my expertise and successful track record to various companies under the name Fisher Consulting. It proved fascinating to observe the current state of these companies and their future expectations. My personal philosophy has always been rooted in conducting a thorough assessment of the present situation and then constructing a clear and visually compelling roadmap towards success. Like a SWOT analysis, this process involves identifying strengths and weaknesses, determining what is currently effective and what is not. To facilitate this, I developed a ten-point scale for my clients, focusing on key elements that would expedite their journey to success. As a consultant, it is important to demonstrate immediate impact and measurable change in everything you do. While some consultants may provide directions and leave the implementation to the client, I remained actively involved throughout the implementation process, conducting regular review meetings to monitor progress. It is vital to ensure that recommendations are executed properly and yield the desired outcomes.

With my background, I had the advantage of examining the entire product development process, from customer channels to customer satisfaction. This enabled me to easily assess the current sales and marketing plan and propose enhancements. However, I needed to be cautious about undermining their existing plan. Instead, I adopted an approach of making slight adjustments to their plan to drive accelerated sales. By implementing these adjustments, I assigned a percentage of success or failure to each recommendation, providing them with a clear indication of which areas required the most attention.

Initially, I requested data on their new customer reports, as it became evident that there was a systemic issue with both manufacturing and distribution when it came to brand building through new business opportunities. Finding new customers seemed to be a common challenge faced by most companies. The question then arose: how does one reach these new customers? The answer lies in investing money in a lead share program. Cold calling is generally disliked, but if the leads are warm, there is a higher likelihood of pursuing the business. It's important to note that traditional methods such as advertisements in trade magazines are not as effective as they used to be due to technological advancements. Therefore, it becomes necessary to take matters into your own hands and invest in finding innovative ways to build new business. On the distribution side, sales hunters often lack the time as they are busy managing existing accounts, while maintainers are hesitant to approach new prospects due to fear of rejection. Some companies have addressed this issue by accommodating compensation structures to include incentives for generating new business. This approach forces a behavioral change in the sales process and has proven successful in many cases. On the other hand, I also developed a risk assessment for customer retention, analyzing what percentage of the business was at risk. It is important to consider both new business and retention within the same context. Regardless of the industry, there will always be a factor of nonrepetitive business. Identifying these factors is essential, and the only way to offset is through acquiring new customers or expanding further within the existing account base.

Effectively communicating complex concepts in a clear and concise manner, both verbally and in writing, was of utmost importance. To address this, I found that flow charting the proposed changes proved to be the most effective solution. It is important to identify the individuals responsible for implementing the changes and ensure that they take full ownership and are held accountable. This is a common gray area where companies often end up pointing fingers when changes fail to materialize into success. To avoid this, it is essential to assign specific individuals or teams to each change initiative. Another critical aspect of communication is the follow-up during the implementation stages. Each stage should be evaluated, and any issues or challenges should be addressed promptly to facilitate progress to the next stage of adaptation. It is advisable to maintain a diary documenting each change, which should be written and signed off on, allowing for the measurement of the internal impact of the changes.

Possessing strong problem-solving skills is essential for effectively addressing the challenges faced by clients. It requires critical thinking, the ability to identify root causes, and the development of innovative solutions to resolve issues. Every action taken elicits a reaction, and it is important for my clients to witness prompt problem resolution throughout the process. In such instances, we often referred to the specific flow chart related to the change and analyzed where our original thinking might have been flawed or identified any unknown factors that might have caused a disruption in the conversion. This analysis allowed us to quickly identify the reasons behind the issue and recommend necessary changes. It is important to remember that as a consultant, the objective is to implement changes that will enhance the company. There may be unforeseen factors uncovered along the way that can potentially hinder the success of the change campaign.

In the ever-evolving cleaning industry, you must be adaptable and flexible to stay abreast of the changes. The client's willingness to embrace new ideas, their openness to learning, and their ability to adjust their strategies accordingly are key factors for success. Before accepting a consulting engagement, it is important to conduct an interview with the potential client to gain a better understanding of their leadership and their receptiveness to change. If there is a sense that the client poses a high risk with low potential rewards, it is essential to have an honest conversation with them, expressing reservations about taking on the job. Essentially, if the client's interview process indicates that they are not fully committed to implementing the necessary changes and may set the project up for failure, it is best to avoid investing their money and to prevent potential pushback against the recommended changes.

My approach has always been to prioritize the needs, goals, and corporate objectives of my clients. To achieve this, I conducted extensive research on their business standing within the industry, analyzing factors such as industry dynamics and challenges. This allowed me to provide tailored solutions that specifically addressed their unique requirements. Just like in sales, thorough preparation is imperative. The more prepared and knowledgeable you are about your client, the higher the chances of success in establishing a mutually beneficial relationship. I have always focused on playing the percentages, even developing a calculator to assess the areas of preparation and provide a success percentage based on the answers to specific questions. Another AI possibility in the future.

To ensure effective project management, I made a conscious effort to limit the number of simultaneous projects worked on. While this can be challenging if consulting is your sole source of income, it is important to effectively manage time, set priorities, and deliver projects within the agreed-upon deadlines. Larger consulting firms have the advantage of dedicated personnel teams that help expedite the implementation of necessary changes for clients.

Maintaining ethical conduct is of utmost importance, and one effective way to ensure this is by signing a nondisclosure agreement (NDA). I strongly recommend that every company adopts this as a standard practice, as it protects both parties from potential misunderstandings that can lead to disruptions. By having a confidentiality agreement in place, conflicts of interest can be avoided, and both parties can act in each other's best interests.

I have always been committed to continuous learning. The cleaning industry is constantly evolving, and I have made it a priority to stay updated with the latest industry trends and engage in professional development activities. It is crucial to examine the successes of other companies, as they often have key components that contribute to their achievements. By identifying these components, we can strive to enhance them for the benefit of our clients. Sometimes, it is necessary to look beyond our industry to find answers. I have always sought inspiration from companies outside of our industry, studying their structures and business delivery systems. Through this approach, I have discovered numerous ideas that can be successfully applied within our industry.

I firmly believe that establishing strong relationships with clients and stakeholders is essential for achieving success. It is important to build trust, foster effective collaboration, and effectively manage relationships with diverse individuals and teams. Conducting a thorough interview process during the client prescreening stage can provide valuable insights and help determine the potential trajectory of the client relationship.

Interestingly, my consulting experience eventually led me back to the manufacturer, where I assumed the role of president.

Lessons Learned

- Create clear and visually compelling roadmaps.
- To persuade someone is to skillfully guide them towards adopting an idea as their own.
- The primary challenge faced by companies is generating new business. Warm leads can help alleviate the fear of cold calling.
- Embrace change, understand its potential, and capitalize on the opportunities it presents.
- Explore beyond your industry for innovative solutions.

CHAPTER 11

UNFINISHED BUSINESS

One day, Larry, the owner, and Michelle, EVP of Human Resources, reached out to me, mentioning that they were in the process of transitioning to new leadership and wanted to discuss a potential role with me. At that time, I had just started my consulting business and was uncertain about returning to the day-to-day responsibilities of a full-time position. However, after careful consideration and recognizing the immense potential, I decided to accept the offer. I was excited to join an exceptional team of professionals.

This experience reminded me of the importance of leaving a company on good terms, maintaining a professional demeanor throughout the process. It's important to remember that you never know what opportunities may arise in the future. Many individuals, driven by frustration, burn bridges when leaving a company, often without considering the potential consequences. Before jeopardizing future opportunities, it's essential to take a step back and think about the long-term implications of our actions.

Stepping back into the plant felt like a homecoming. I was greeted by familiar faces like Kevin, Matt, and Terese, who had been dedicated associates of the company for a long time. However, there were also many new faces, as it had been seventeen years since I'd left to start my own business. Retirement and changing times had brought about significant changes. Now, it was time to rebuild and focus on growth!

The leadership team consisted of a diverse group of talented individuals. What intrigued me was their strong belief in the EOS process, an operating system I was familiar with from my experience. I knew firsthand the benefits of having a well-informed, structured, and organized team.

Early on, I noticed that the company seemed to be stuck in a rut. Despite having a wealth of innovation and quality equipment, we lacked a strong position in the marketplace. The previous personnel had done an excellent job of building simple, reliable, and durable equipment, but they struggled to effectively communicate that message to the industry. While the branding appeared good, the company faced challenges in conveying it properly to the masses.

It was intriguing to reenter the manufacturing side and observe the companies that had thrived, while others remained stagnant or became nonviable. After seventeen years, I noticed familiar faces still occupying the same positions. In the Sanitary Maintenance industry, it seemed that once people entered, they rarely left, and if they did, they often found their way back. Time had passed, and we were all growing older.

I embarked on a period of introspection to determine if my new associates were open to change. Did they possess the desire to break free from the status quo and become a prominent player in the industry? We needed a transformation. While there were skeptics initially, they soon realized that I had returned with the intention of winning, not settling for second or third place. It was critical for everyone in the organization to recognize and embrace our potential as a company. I made it clear that we all needed to roll up our sleeves and give it our all.

I swiftly evaluated our frontline sales team to determine if we had the best individuals in each territory. It is often said that you are only as strong as your weakest link in the field. While achieving 100 percent excellence may be unrealistic, we aimed to start by setting our sights on reaching 65-70 percent of the best salespeople. Once we built momentum and established our brand, we would naturally attract exceptional representatives who wanted to work for our organization. Ultimately, it becomes a matter of financial opportunity-can they make significant earnings by selling our equipment? The saying, "if you build it, they will come" holds true for any organization. With this in mind, we revamped our sales force and bolstered the overall group. We enlisted experienced sales managers and began charting an innovation roadmap towards success.

The challenge we faced was how to gain market share in a mature market. To outperform our competition, we needed to think ahead and find creative ways to make significant leaps, rather than incremental steps. In the next chapter, you will discover how we swiftly pivoted the business, turning what many of our competitors considered their worst year into a triumph for us, achieving a remarkable gain of over 25 percent.

We recognized the need to expand and enhance our existing marketing platform. To gain recognition in any industry, it is essential to make your presence known. We needed to take our message to social media and to the streets. Our equipment, which was truly the best in the industry, had never received the spotlight it deserved. We were determined not to leave behind a legacy of being overlooked. I wanted to personally witness the impact of our marketing efforts. I vividly remember on customer visitations supervisors and managers of facilities expressing their surprise, asking why they had never heard of our equipment before, as it was the best they had seen in a long time. Returning to the company, I shook my head in disbelief, realizing that we had a hidden gem. All we needed to do was uncover its shine and polish it every day.

Our operations and engineering departments were staffed with exceptional associates who possess incredible talent. It was disheartening to see that their innovations and improvements fell short of disserved expectations. This had to change because the key to overcoming our challenges and moving forward was to drive revenue growth through innovation. To achieve this, we devised comprehensive plans.

Firstly, we increased our investment in new product development, ensuring that our offerings were at the forefront of the industry. We also revamped our marketing approach, emphasizing that we offered the best scrubbers available. To back up this claim, we introduced the best warranty in the industry. Additionally, we enhanced our field support and developed a special markets program to supplement distributor growth.

In our engineering department, we adopted a simple yet powerful principle: listening to the voice of the customer. We focused on building machines that catered to the specific needs of our customers. We invested time and effort in actively seeking input from those working in the field, allowing us to establish measurable benchmarks that contributed to the production of successful machines.

The sanitary maintenance industry faced a significant influx of equipment imports from China and Europe. This is not to discredit our competitors, but we firmly believe that we build superior machines and offer better cleaning solutions. Unfortunately, the industry became complacent and developed a misconception about price. Many believed that buying cheaper equipment would lead to higher profits. However, in today's business landscape, there will always be someone offering a cheaper price for a product. If you solely focus on competing on price, you will eventually lose your unique identity.

Our concept was straightforward: we produce the best machines on the market, and customers are willing to pay for quality and reliability. We emphasized the importance of making a wise investment by understanding the total cost of ownership. While the imports may have led to the commoditization of the equipment category, we remained steadfast in our commitment to offering superior products.

In any industry, when imports drive prices down to enter the American market, essentially buying their way in, and when coupled with a polluted distribution channel, the market experiences severe margin erosion. It is important to remember the adage that you are what you price and promote. We aimed to differentiate ourselves by focusing on quality, reliability, and the overall value our machines provided, rather than engaging in a race to the bottom on price.

We firmly believe that having a high-quality product and the ability to deliver better than anyone else in the business creates a winning combination. Our operational team has always been proactive in staying ahead of the curve, monitoring external trends that could impact components and potential shortages. This foresight has allowed us to win over many customers who were unable to obtain products from their primary sources. The response from their customers has been along the lines of, "Why didn't you show us this equipment before you sold us the other brand?" We have successfully capitalized on our speed to market concept, and our quick ship program has been particularly beneficial for building service contractors who require products for start-ups.

In terms of our plant, we have assembled the best production team in the industry. Our HR department and VP of operations have done an exceptional job in building an unbeatable team. Under the guidance of Teresa, the production team consistently goes above and beyond to make things happen. I have witnessed their ability to respond to large orders and, to my surprise, beat deadlines. Engaging with the plant personnel through activities such as golf, bowling, lunches, and dinners is an enjoyable part of the business for me. It allows me to get to know and bond with our front-line associates. The excitement when I walk the plant floor is radiating.

We recognized the need to align our marketing strategy with the prevailing narrative. Previously, the company had been attempting to compete on price in the market. However, we shifted our approach; it is not about pricing it, but rather effectively selling it. To achieve this, we began developing technology to assist our customers in differentiating themselves based on the value of the product they were selling.

Our approach involved providing return on investment tools that supported the concept of total cost of ownership. By simplifying the process of selling a premium product and equipping our customers with easily accessible tools to enhance their knowledge, we increased the likelihood of successful sales. Empowering their customers with the information needed to make informed decisions regarding capital expenses became our distinguishing factor. We started branding ourselves as a premium product that could be easily justified in terms of investment cost.

In many cases, there is a disconnect between the group expressing interest, the group making the purchase, and the group responsible for financial approval. Without proper knowledge, it may seem logical to opt for the cheapest machine. However, this often leads to higher costs in the long run. We understood the power of information and recognized that how it is distributed and managed can greatly impact the return on investment, making every dollar spent on acquiring that information worthwhile.

We have taken a new approach to branding our company, one that embraces laughter and fun. It all began with establishing a theme at our national convention, centered around competition, and striving for excellence in one's profession. We decided to integrate sports with cleaning, creating a unique and engaging concept.

In 2022, we launched a social media campaign focused on boxing, where we proudly coined the phrase, "Undisputed Champion of Clean," which we have since trademarked. Through humorous posts, we compared our equipment and cleaning solutions to a heavyweight champion, effectively conveying the message of our superiority. At the convention that year, our booth was designed as a boxing ring, and our booth participants dressed as trainers. The show was a tremendous success, and attendees eagerly anticipated what we had in store for 2023.

That year in May was a significant turning point in my life. At the time, I was not feeling well, and during my annual physical, my doctor expressed concern about the noticeable increase in my PSA blood results. He assured me that he would connect me with the top urologist in the Midwest. A meeting was arranged, and I underwent an examination. The doctor then informed me that the next step would be a biopsy, which was subsequently scheduled and completed.

The memory of the day I received the news of my cancer diagnosis will forever stay with me. I was attending a trade show when I had to excuse myself to take the call. The doctor informed me that the results were not favorable but emphasized that we had caught it early. He advised me to schedule an appointment to see him upon my return. Strangely, this news did not seem to affect me much. I had a strong sense of determination and was ready to face any challenges that lay ahead. So, I rejoined my business associates at the show as if nothing had happened.

When I returned, I went to see the doctor; he laid out the options. He said if it were him, he would remove the prostate. So, we set up the prostatectomy for July 7. On my way to the operating room, I inquired about my doctor. The nurses replied, "You are in good hands," as they referred to him as a superstar. It took me three months to recover, but it did not deter me as I worked right through it. I had a catheter, had to change my nutrition and physical activity. It was painful as I refused any pain medication, and the scares from the robot-assisted radical prostatectomy (RARP) were the worse part. As I went for my morning walks, I kept telling myself this was just a bump in the road, it would all be in the rear-view mirror soon. The results from the operation were successful and my margins were excellent; the chance it had spread was minimal. I recall going to see the doctor after the operation, and he was ecstatic that my PSA was negligible. He was more excited about it than me, and that's when I knew I was in good hands; he cared about his patients. We had scheduled meetings every three months to monitor the PSA. Six months after the prostatectomy, my PSA had crept back up, so there was obviously something still there. He said it was time he passed me on to an oncologist to discuss next steps, most likely radiation.

When I met with the oncologist, her initial suggestion was to continue monitoring my PSA for a few more months before considering radiation. She wanted to avoid radiation if it wasn't necessary. Unfortunately, the PSA reached a level that both of us agreed indicated it was time for radiation. I embarked on a thirty-five-day radiation treatment journey, with the oncologist joking that we would be best friends during that time, but she hoped to not see me again afterward. Before each radiation session, I had to drink a significant amount of water to ensure my bladder was full. This process was both humbling and humiliating, as without a prostate, it was challenging to control my bladder, leading to occasional accidents. However, I remained determined to beat the disease and continued working as if it was business as usual throughout the thirty-five days. One of the most rewarding aspects of this experience was the connections I formed with fellow fighters, John, and Bill, whom I met before and after my radiation sessions. We became close friends, had several lunch meetings to discuss life, family, and the joys of being grandparents. We made plans to get together for a golf outing once the weather improved.

Although I hope my battle with this deadly disease is over, if it resurfaces, I am prepared to face it with the same unwavering determination. It will not change or impact my life, and I will not allow it to win.

Later that year, we kicked off a training theme, featuring Harry and Monty from the Major League as our MCs. We incorporated various characters from baseball movies, tying them to our products and cleaning. The baseball theme has been well-received, as people appreciate doing business with individuals who think creatively. Our customers and partners are already speculating about the theme for 2024, as we continue to make doing business with us enjoyable and rewarding.

By infusing our branding efforts with humor and excitement, we are creating a memorable and engaging experience for all involved.

Our approach is outward-focused, always seeking solutions for our customers, even if it doesn't directly result in the sale of our products. A prime example of this is when we had a large customer tasked with eliminating burnishing while still achieving a shiny floor. We recognized that the only way to accomplish this was through a combination of chemicals, abrasives, and machines. We took the initiative to combine and test this concept, and it proved to be the answer, ultimately saving the customer millions of dollars.

I have long advocated for the importance of cleaning systems. It is important to have the right system in place that consistently delivers the desired outcome. When there is a disjointed approach to the cleaning process, it becomes all too common for everyone involved to start pointing fingers when the desired outcome is not achieved. This is a daily occurrence in our industry. We were among the first in the industry to prioritize simple systems that consistently provided superior outcomes over an extended period. While we may not always secure equipment sales, our customers recognize that we are the ones who brought them a simplified system, eliminating the need to outsource what was perceived as a complicated method.

Our commitment to finding solutions and simplifying processes has earned us the trust and loyalty of our customers. We understand that our success lies not only in selling products but also in providing comprehensive solutions that meet their unique needs.

We recognized the need to explore autonomous cleaning and began researching companies that were experimenting with cleaning machines. However, many of our competitors hastily jumped on board with a single software company just to claim they had an autonomous machine, without selling any. We made a conscious decision to divert our investment elsewhere.

The challenge with wet scrubbing is that floors are often not preswept, resulting in debris being picked up by the unmanned scrubbing machine's squeegee. This leads to streaks and excessive water on the floor, creating a safety hazard for slips and falls. Can a cleaner truly be eliminated, or do they still need to manually mop, fill, and empty the unit, and charge it? During my extensive travels and interactions with customers, I often ask proud owners of autonomous machines two questions: how frequently do they run the machine in manual mode, and how quickly can they get the machine operational when it breaks down? Often, the responses reveal that the machine is used in manual mode over 50 percent of the time. I then point out that they are essentially paying four times the cost for a machine that their cleaners are still operating manually. Is that truly a wise investment?

As an organization, we chose to observe from the sidelines, witnessing the mistakes and misfortunes of buyers. While we acknowledge that the technology is advancing, we have taken a different approach. Rather than simply investing money to join the autonomous game and say, "Look at us," we have focused on changing the entire game. We have many new products in development that address the specific needs of our customers before we venture into autonomous cleaning. Sometimes, it is necessary to take a step back and observe before rushing to be the first. Otherwise, it can become a costly proposition.

I recall a humorous incident when I visited one of my competitors' booths and asked why they didn't have an autonomous scrubber with the squeegee down, wet scrubbing the floor. The competitor laughed and admitted they were aware of the challenges. This made me question the purpose of having technology if you are afraid or ill-equipped to sell it. We believe in being fully prepared and equipped to provide effective solutions to our customers before embracing new technologies.

We are incredibly fortunate to have achieved the remarkable feat of doubling the size of our business within a span of three years. Larry, our owner, possesses a clear vision of our trajectory and is making substantial investments to propel our growth. One significant step we have taken is doubling the size of our manufacturing facility, positioning ourselves for a promising future. With the introduction of new innovative products and our unwavering commitment to building our brand, we are confident that the rewards will extend to future generations.

To truly understand our determination and resilience, let's rewind to March of 2020 when the devastating impact of the pandemic began to unfold. Despite the challenging circumstances, we remained steadfast in our pursuit of success.

Lessons Learned

- Always strive to leave a job on excellent terms and express gratitude for the opportunities it provided you.

- If you have a great product, find ways to transform it into a phenomenal success story.

- Invest in customer research and feedback to uncover valuable insights and opportunities for growth.

- Winning together, there is no better feeling.

- Building your brand should be an enjoyable and exhilarating experience for your customers.

- Offer solutions to problems, even if there is no immediate personal gain.

CHAPTER 12

COVID-19

The arrival of COVID-19 in the United States in March 2020 had profound and far-reaching consequences across multiple sectors. The pandemic's impact was felt not only in public health but also in the economy, education, and various aspects of daily life. As the situation unfolded, it became evident that a comprehensive response was necessary to address the challenges posed by the virus.

In the early days of March 2020, the world was caught off-guard by the rapid spread of the virus and the severity of its impact. The pandemic hit hard and fast, leaving governments, businesses, and individuals scrambling to adapt to the new reality. The immediate focus was on implementing public health measures to slow the spread of the virus and protect vulnerable populations.

However, these necessary measures, such as lockdowns, travel restrictions, and social distancing, had a profound impact on the global economy. The closure of businesses, job losses, and a significant decline in economic activity became widespread. Industries that heavily relied on in-person interactions, such as tourism, hospitality, and retail, were particularly hard-hit.

The economic consequences of the pandemic were devastating, with many businesses struggling to survive and millions of people facing unemployment or reduced income. Governments around the world implemented various economic support measures to mitigate the impact, including stimulus packages, grants, and loans to businesses, and expanded unemployment benefits.

In addition to the economic fallout, the pandemic also had significant social and mental health impacts. The isolation caused by lockdowns and social distancing measures took a toll on individuals' mental well-being. Schools and universities had to adapt to remote learning, disrupting the education system and affecting students' academic progress.

As the situation evolved, efforts were made to address these challenges. Vaccine development and distribution became a top priority, with governments and pharmaceutical companies working together to expedite the process. Ongoing research and collaboration aimed to understand the virus better and develop effective treatments.

While the early days of March 2020 were marked by uncertainty and the devastating impact of the pandemic, it also brought forth a collective determination to overcome the challenges. The resilience and adaptability demonstrated by individuals, communities, and organizations was remarkable, and the ongoing efforts to combat the virus and its consequences continued to shape our response to this unprecedented global crisis.

I rejoined my company in October of 2019 with a clear vision to grow the business. However, when March 2020 arrived, the world was suddenly thrust into a completely different reality. I vividly remember sitting in my hotel room, feeling the impact of the pandemic as my primary hotel downtown closed its doors. It was a moment that forced us to think quickly and strategically about how we could survive the devastating economic downturn.

During this challenging situation, I reached out to a manufacturing company that specialized in producing foaming machines for the food processing industry. To my surprise, they were already exploring the development of a sprayer. What intrigued me about their design was its wide-area coverage capability. Unlike the standard handheld units that required constant refilling, this unit boasted a fifteen-gallon capacity and was equipped with a compressor, allowing for disinfection of surfaces up to 150 feet away from the base. It was a perfect fit for our business model, as it significantly reduced the time spent on the task by utilizing a mechanized system.

Recognizing the potential of this innovative product, we swiftly incorporated it into our product offering. Over the next four months, we sold over 3,500 units, a remarkable achievement considering the circumstances. Additionally, this success allowed us to explore other products that were considered essential in the current climate.

By adapting to the changing market demands and seizing the opportunity presented by this wide-area sprayer, we not only survived the economic downturn but thrived. Our ability to identify and embrace products that aligned with our business model and addressed the emerging needs of our customers played a pivotal role in our success during these challenging times.

We remained committed to staying agile and responsive to the ever-evolving market landscape. We continued to seek out innovative solutions that not only met the demands of the present but also positioned us for future growth and resilience. The lessons learned from this experience have reinforced our belief in the power of adaptability and the importance of seizing opportunities, even in the face of adversity.

During this period, we recognized the importance of addressing both airborne and surface protection to meet the evolving needs of our customers. To provide comprehensive solutions, we established partnerships with UV companies, enabling us to offer a range of options for disinfection. As the scientific understanding shifted towards the significance of airborne exposure, our sales experienced diverse growth.

To further support businesses during uncertain times, we decided to create a subsidiary called Pure Protective Equipment. This new venture aimed to assist organizations in navigating the challenges by offering a roadmap of integrated preventative disinfection systems and technologies. Our goal was to enhance and strengthen their cleaning, sanitizing, and disinfecting processes.

With a focus on keeping businesses safe, healthy, and operational, Pure Protective Equipment assembled a team of forward-thinking individuals. Together, we were dedicated to delivering cutting-edge technological advancements in cleaning equipment. Our solutions were proven to reduce labor hours while achieving rapid and effective results, leading to significant productivity gains for our clients.

By combining their expertise in disinfection technologies with our commitment to driving the sales and marketing, Pure Protective Equipment became a trusted partner for businesses seeking reliable and efficient cleaning solutions. We understood the importance of staying ahead of the curve and continuously improved our offerings to meet the ever-changing demands of the market.

Pure Protective Equipment remained committed to providing businesses with the tools and knowledge they needed to maintain a safe and healthy environment. We continued to invest, ensuring that our products and services remained at the forefront of the industry.

In an all-hands-on-deck approach to rebuilding our country stronger than ever before, companies joined forces with Pure Protective Equipment, serving as the launching pad to propel facilities forward and conquer the uncertainties that lay ahead. Together, we are committed to creating a safer and healthier environment by ensuring the surfaces we touch and the air we breathe are protected.

To expand our offerings and address the challenges posed by the pandemic, we strategically added six companies to our portfolio, each providing a unique solution to combat the threat. This diversification allowed us to meet the diverse needs of our customers and cater to their immediate peace of mind. The response was overwhelming.

Recognizing the importance of educating our representatives to effectively sell these solutions, we appointed a leader, Mike, who had previous experience in the healthcare industry, to oversee our PPE division. This ensured that our team was well-equipped to communicate the value and benefits of our new products to our customers.

Our success is a testament to the trust and confidence our customers have placed in us. We are grateful for their support and remain committed to delivering exceptional products and services that exceed their expectations. As we move forward, we will continue to innovate, adapt, and provide the necessary tools and knowledge to help businesses thrive in the face of uncertainty.

In response to the cancellation of our national trade show, we took the initiative to create a virtual trade fair called Clean Expo 2020. This innovative approach allowed us to connect with customers and potential clients through virtual booths, replicating the experience of an in-person exhibition. We were thrilled to have over three hundred visitors participate in the show, engaging in conversations and attending training breakout sessions. The success of the event exceeded our expectations, capturing the interest of many attendees and resulting in an excellent return on our initial investment.

However, amidst the triumphs and growth we experienced during this time, it is important to acknowledge the devastating impact of the pandemic. The public health crisis caused by the virus led to the loss of millions of lives and overwhelmed healthcare systems worldwide. Tragically, my close friend and business associate of thirty-five years, Paul, lost his life to the pandemic. His passing was a profound loss for our industry, as he was not only an ambassador but also a source of laughter, success, and positivity. Paul's absence is deeply felt, and his presence would have undoubtedly contributed to the growth and achievements we are currently experiencing. He deserved to witness and be a part of this journey, but it was not in our hands as the Lord had other plans.

As we navigated the challenging times, we honored Paul's memory and the impact he had on our lives and industry. We strive to carry forward his spirit of positivity, resilience, and friendship. Though his physical presence may be missed, his legacy lives on in our hearts and in the laughter and successes we continue to share.

The closure of schools and universities worldwide had a significant impact on education. Students were forced to adapt to remote learning, presenting challenges for those without access to technology or reliable Internet connections. Beyond the academic disruptions, the closure of educational institutions has also had social and emotional consequences for students.

Recognizing the need to support the reopening of schools and restore a sense of normalcy, we took the initiative to design a re-opening roadmap. To address the concerns and challenges faced by schools, we authored a white paper that provided solutions for every aspect of the schools' blueprint. As cleaning equipment is a primary source of revenue for us, we understood the importance of offering solutions that prioritized the safety and well-being of the student population.

To further emphasize the significance of our solutions, we developed a student absentee calculator. This tool considered existing absenteeism and calculated the potential additional funding that school districts could receive by implementing proper disinfection measures and reducing absenteeism rates. It is worth noting that school funding is often based on absentee records, making it crucial to prioritize the health and safety of students.

Unfortunately, it was ironic that a significant portion of the federal funds allocated for protective devices and equipment was diverted to other pressing needs. While we were able to capitalize on some projects and funding opportunities, most of the money was spent in other areas. This lack of accountability in the use of funds specifically designated for the health and safety of the environment is a concern that I have often pondered.

The funding I am referring to came from various sources, including FEMA, the Education Stabilization Act (CARES), and ESSER funds. It is disheartening to witness the misallocation of resources meant to protect and support our educational institutions during these challenging times. It is important that we advocate for greater transparency and accountability in the use of funds, ensuring that they are directed towards the intended purpose of safeguarding the health and safety of our students and educational environments.

To mitigate the spread of the virus, various measures such as stay-at-home orders, business closures, and restrictions on gatherings were implemented. These actions had a profound impact on our daily lives, disrupting work routines, educational systems, and social activities. Numerous events, conferences, and sports leagues were either canceled or postponed indefinitely.

Fortunately, our classification as an essential business allowed us to continue producing products that played a vital role in preventing the spread of the virus. This designation provided us with the opportunity to contribute to the collective effort of safeguarding public health. Our Human Resources department played a pivotal role in keeping our workforce united and engaged during this transition. They successfully facilitated the shift to remote work capabilities, allowing employees to work from the safety and comfort of their homes.

Throughout this challenging period, our team demonstrated resilience, adaptability, and a commitment to supporting one another. We are grateful for the dedication and efforts of our employees, who have played an integral role in helping us weather the storm and continue serving our customers. As we move forward, we remain committed to prioritizing the health and well-being of our team.

The global pandemic also caused significant disruptions to supply chains worldwide, resulting in shortages of essential goods and medical supplies. This highlighted the vulnerability of international trade and the interconnectedness of economies, as countries struggled to secure the necessary resources and equipment.

Recognizing the potential impact of these shortages, our supply chain management team proactively anticipated the crisis and took measures to stay ahead of it. This allowed us to have a sufficient supply of equipment once commercial and institutional buildings began to reopen. As a result, we positioned ourselves as the go-to "Quick Ship" company, providing prompt and reliable delivery of products. This reputation has remained with us to this day.

Our production team played a major role in our success, excelling in every aspect of servicing our customers. Their dedication and efficiency allowed us to meet the demands of our clients and gain the trust of large customers. As facilities started using our equipment, they were pleasantly surprised by its simplicity, durability, and reliability. This positive feedback opened doors of opportunity for our company, further expanding our reach and impact.

Having a reliable supply of equipment not only ensured our customers' satisfaction but also enabled us to seize new opportunities in the market. By being well-prepared and having the necessary resources, we were able to meet the needs of our customers and contribute to their success.

The global pandemic had a profound impact on domestic and international travel, resulting in travel restrictions and border closures. Flights were canceled, and stringent quarantine measures were implemented to mitigate the spread of the virus.

I vividly remember the disappointment I experienced when the pandemic affected my plans to attend InterClean. I had a full week of meetings scheduled and was eagerly looking forward to reconnecting with long-term friends and business associates. However, as I checked with the airline, I learned about the new travel requirements. Since I was not vaccinated, I needed to provide a negative test result and a letter from my doctor confirming that I had previously contracted COVID and was immune to the virus. Unfortunately, the travel restrictions had changed, particularly for entry into the Netherlands, and I had no choice but to cancel my flight.

Although the frustration and disappointment were palpable, I now realize that it may have been a blessing in disguise. A colleague of mine who attended the show contracted COVID while in the Netherlands and had to undergo a seven-day quarantine with negative test results before being allowed to reenter the United States. Considering this, it is possible that being turned away from the trip spared me from potential health risks and further disruptions.

While the cancellation of my trip was undoubtedly disappointing, I recognized the importance of prioritizing health and safety during these uncertain times. I remained hopeful that in the future, I would have the opportunity to visit my friends and colleagues once again. Until then, I continued to adapt and find alternative ways to maintain connections and foster business relationships in a safe and responsible manner.

Throughout the pandemic, we prioritized driving new product development by assembling a dedicated team of creative individuals who consistently engaged in brainstorming sessions and generated innovative ideas. By fostering a culture that values creativity and encourages thinking outside the box, we ensured that our product pipeline remained vibrant with exciting concepts.

Recognizing the urgency of the situation, with many of our competitors facing operational challenges, we implemented an aggressive new product roadmap. Leveraging our advanced technologies, we swiftly transformed ideas into tangible prototypes. This allowed us to expedite the testing and refinement process, enabling us to bring our products to market at an accelerated pace.

We understood that in times of uncertainty, innovation becomes even more crucial. By proactively investing in our creative team and leveraging our technological capabilities, we were able to stay ahead of the curve and meet the evolving needs of our customers. Our commitment to driving new product development remains unwavering, as we strive to deliver cutting-edge solutions that make a positive impact in the market.

To gather valuable insights, we conducted numerous virtual focus groups, demonstrating our commitment to listening to the voice of the customer. We firmly believe that collaboration is key to success, which is why we established strategic product meetings with our customers. By leveraging their expertise and insights, we tapped into a wealth of knowledge and ensured that our products were truly groundbreaking.

Fortunately, our strategic decisions and actions positioned us favorably for future growth. While many of our competitors experienced a significant decline in their overall business during 2020, we were fortunate to achieve a healthy increase over the previous year. The decisions, made under challenging business conditions, not only allowed us to weather the storm but also enabled us to gain valuable market share.

We are proud of the choices we made during this difficult period, as they have proven to be instrumental in our success. By staying focused on innovation and adapting to the changing landscape, we were able to differentiate ourselves from the competition and position ourselves for continued growth.

As we move forward, we remain committed to maintaining our momentum and capitalizing on the opportunities that lie ahead. We will continue to prioritize innovation, customer satisfaction, and strategic decision-making to ensure our continued success in the market.

Lessons Learned

- Don't get complacent and instead be proactive in addressing future health crises.
- During times of mass confusion, such as a pandemic, it is important to step back, assess the situation, and work towards your contribution to resolving the issues at hand.
- Be quick and decisive in your resolve.
- Bring collective innovation together to solve issues.
- Eliminate fear by providing direction.

CHAPTER 13

INNOVATION SELLS

Innovative products can be defined as those that provide enhanced functionality, increased efficiency, a competitive advantage, improved user experience, sustainability, adaptability, and the potential for market leadership.

Embracing innovation can bring substantial benefits to businesses and consumers alike. In my forty-two years of experience in the cleaning industry, I have witnessed several innovations that have had a significant impact in the equipment category. However, I do not intend to discount the importance of innovations in other categories.

In this chapter, I will focus on several innovations that have made a major impact on both soft and hard surface flooring compositions.

Carpet Care Innovations

The first innovation I want to highlight is a two-motor upright vacuum cleaner that competed against single-motor models priced four times higher. It may have seemed unimaginable at the time, but this unit not only sold well but also became a trailblazer for years to come. It stands to reason that having two motors would provide better performance. Additionally, the unit featured on-board accessory tools for convenient cleaning of hard-to-reach areas and dusting. The handle weight was light, and the electronics ensured the customers' investment was protected.

The carpet mills were highly supportive of this innovation because the unit effectively picked up dry contaminants and reduced warranty claims for prematurely worn-out carpets. Investing in a unit that would revolutionize the way people vacuumed floors in commercial and institutional applications was a significant change. However, the specific mission of this launch was clear: to provide cleaner carpets, faster cleaning (reducing labor), and eliminate premature wear.

This successful product, which I am proud to say I was a part of, also led to the development of a sister vacuum, which has become the best-selling vacuum in the commercial market. It is highly likely that you will find this vacuum in every hotel you stay in. This example demonstrates that an innovative product not only brings additional products but also truly sells well. Innovation truly drives success in the market.

This company had the foresight to revolutionize the cleaning industry by introducing a vacuum that could be worn on the back of a worker. This innovative approach set a new standard and was specifically developed for the contracting business to reduce labor. By utilizing a wand and a carefully designed process, the productivity rate was significantly improved. The company was based in an area known for hiking, and they leveraged their knowledge to create a comfortable backpack vacuum with weight evenly distributed throughout a harness. The success of this product offering allowed the company to expand its range with other innovative products. Clearly, innovation sells!

Interestingly, both companies were not the first to introduce battery-powered units and eliminate cords. They followed the lead of others. This highlights the importance of companies pushing boundaries and breaking down barriers. Sometimes, it is necessary for one company to pave the way, allowing others to capitalize on the initial innovation and develop further on existing technologies.

The market saw the introduction of autonomous vacuums, and it is interesting to note that these innovations originated from overseas. While these vacuums did reduce labor to some extent, there were still tasks such as changing bags, setting up charging, and cleaning out the brush for optimal performance. Someone will inevitably take the risk and break through that barrier, even if it means facing challenges along the way. I believe that other companies will benefit from the initial exposure and learn from these innovations. After all, innovation sells!

It is pivotal to acknowledge that unless you are willing to make a risky investment, your innovation is likely to remain shelved. I have witnessed numerous great ideas that never made it to market. I can recall a personal experience where we were leaders in upright vacuums, but another company beat us with backpack models. I had the idea to shift the weight of the backpack to the hip, which made sense. Our engineers at the time agreed it was a great idea, but believed we wouldn't have enough space for a vacuum and disposable bag to implement it. However, a few years later, a company introduced the Hip Vac, proving that our concept was indeed viable. Unfortunately, another product, the battery backpack was displayed at our industry trade show in 1999 by our company, ahead of its time, as the components for a reliable product were not yet available. Our soft launch went nowhere, only to see the market fully embrace the cordless concept later.

For those who have been in the industry cleaning industry for a while, you can surely recall the old box and wand extractor, which involved a labor-intensive process to extract soil from carpets, commonly known as carpet extraction. Interestingly, there were two companies that both claimed to be the first to invent the self-contained extractor. Just imagine looking at the box and wand, power brush or wand, and envisioning a way to combine all those components to drastically enhance productivity. While the self-contained extractor did not completely replace the box and wand, it did shift the box and wand use from commercial and institutional markets to becoming a tool utilized by the professional carpet cleaner.

The birth of the self-contained extractor resulted in various shapes and sizes of machines. Nowadays, if you rent a unit to clean your carpets at home, chances are it will be self-contained and easy to use. However, it wasn't always like that. The introduction of one-pass cleaning revolutionized the carpet extraction process. This example once again demonstrates that innovation sells and can transform an industry.

During the old days when carpets were wool or a wool blend, a company introduced an innovative approach to carpet cleaning by utilizing dry compounds. This method gained the endorsement of carpet mills because it avoided over-wetting the carpets. The company seized the opportunity and became a leader in the dry-cleaning system. However, they were unaware that once the mills completed their transition to nylon fibers, the need for dry turned to the wet concept of rinsing carpets as the recommended method. This serves as a prime example of the importance of measuring the longevity of an innovation. Once the wet concept became the preferred method for carpet cleaning, the company's success dwindled, unintentionally, no pun intended, drying up their business.

However, this movement in carpet cleaning gave rise to a new and faster approach to achieving the same outcome. The emergence of low moisture cleaning, known as carpet encapsulation, came into the spotlight. This led equipment companies to develop delivery systems specifically designed for the low moisture crystallization process. The technology involved driving the low moisture crystals into the carpet to bond with dirt, which could then encapsulate the dirt, and be vacuumed out dry, similar to the dry compound delivery system. The key difference was that this method proved to be faster. While the dry compound approach was labor-intensive, it had the support of carpet mills in the earlier years of carpet evolution.

What do all carpet cleaning innovations have in common? They share the ability to change the cleaning process, simplify usage, gain third-party endorsements, and reduce labor while still achieving superior results. It is evident that innovation sells!

As time progressed, the size of vacuums and extractors increased to address the need for speed and labor reduction. Larger machines introduced innovative features, although they may not have had the same impact as completely changing the cleaning process.

It is important to understand that simply having an innovation does not guarantee its success in the market. Supporting the process change with evidence, ensuring proper sales techniques, justifying the cost, and executing a well-visualized launch are all essential factors. Unfortunately, a significant percentage of new product innovations fail to reach their fullest potential.

Hard Floor Innovations

The evolution of hard floor care was largely influenced by chemical manufacturers. In the early years of my career, coatings played a significant role in determining the machines required to complete tasks and maintain floors at an acceptable level. Several trailblazers emerged during this time, setting the stage for future generations of copies as well as new technologies.

One unexpected innovation came from a company that I worked for that thought of using a weedwhacker to clean baseboards. This unique addition to the fleet of floor machines proved to be highly beneficial and paved the way for subsequent innovations in the detail cleaning machine category.

Another notable innovation involved transforming a sit-down auto scrubber into a stand-on machine, inspired by the forklift industry. This bold move aimed to set a new standard that others would follow. As the saying goes, being the first to break through the wall often comes with challenges. However, this company overcame any service issues and changed the game by revolutionizing the way floors are cleaned. Today, stand-on versions of floor scrubbers are commonplace, thanks to the trailblazing efforts of this company.

Let's explore the story of a company that had an innovation initially used in a different industry, which eventually crossed over and created a new category in cleaning known as orbital technology. Originally designed for the wood floor industry, particularly gym floors in the educational market, this innovation involved a process that roughed up floors for simple recoating. However, the company began experimenting with the weight of the head and discovered that it could significantly reduce scrubbing and recoating time, and even strip floors under the right conditions.

The industry embraced this initial thrust of orbital technology due to the substantial labor reduction it offered in the process of scrubbing, stripping, and recoating floors. However, the units themselves did not hold up well under those demanding conditions. This led to a frantic race to improve and refine the technology, resulting in the production of scrubbers, floor machines, and detail machines equipped with orbital technology. This advancement propelled companies like the one I currently lead to become leaders in design and performance. Other companies also emerged as niche players in the floor machines and detail markets, capitalizing on the benefits of orbital technology.

The evolution of the cleaning industry has seen significant improvements in productivity, particularly with the introduction of auto scrubbers. In the past, walk-behind scrubbers were the norm, but in the 1980s, riding machines became popular, followed by stand-on versions in the 2000s. Despite these advancements, all these machines relied on wet cell battery technology. While there have been advancements with batteries such as AGM and lithium, wet cell batteries, or also known as lead acid batteries, remained the preferred choice due to their cost and performance. However, one major issue with wet cell batteries is the lack of proper maintenance, resulting in prorated warranties and minimal performance. To address this concern, our company developed a technology called Battery Shield. Our scrubbers were equipped with wet cells that were enclosed with sensors and floats, alerting the operator when the unit needed to be filled with distilled water. Additionally, a light indicator on the control panel notified the operator, and the power to the brush system automatically turned off until the batteries were refreshed. This forced preventive maintenance, ensuring that the operator could not clean the floor before attending to the batteries. We also introduced a hydro-link system that topped off the cells with the precise amount of water, preventing overfilling and potential damage to the batteries. To further protect the filling process, we added a flow meter. This innovation revolutionized maintenance on wet cell batteries in the cleaning industry.

Who would have imagined that combining a pressure washer, wet vacuum, and cleaning tools could revolutionize the way commercial and institutional restrooms are cleaned? Well, it happened, and the company behind this innovative concept has successfully built numerous units based on this platform. As expected, there was a rush to copy the concept, but most attempts were unsuccessful. However, by carefully studying the flaws and understanding why people may be hesitant to use such a tool, it is possible to springboard the concept and deliver another innovation that surpasses expectations.

The invention of the bucket by Thomas Crapper in 1836 revolutionized cleaning practices. In 1893, Thomas W. Steward, an African American inventor, was awarded patent number 499,402 for inventing the mop. Steward's deck mop, made of yarn, quickly gained popularity for household and commercial/institutional cleaning.

Microfiber, a type of polyester with thin filaments, was introduced as an alternative to traditional mops in 1986. Its origins are disputed, with some claiming it was developed by the Japanese in the mid-1970s and others suggesting it was introduced in England in 1986. However, it is certain that Sweden began marketing the first microfiber products in 1990.

In the 1950s, a German company introduced the first micro scrubber, the BS 350, for cleaning confined spaces. Micro scrubbers officially entered the market in the late 2000s, followed by the I-mop shortly after.

All these cleaning units, since the invention of the traditional mop and bucket in the 1890s, aimed to remove soil from confined spaces. While each had its own success, none of them eliminated the need for daily use of the mop bucket and wringer.

Our company just recently introduced the Quick Scrub, a battery-powered unit with the same footprint as a mop and bucket. This innovative device enables operators to clean under fixed tables and equipment in commercial kitchens, as well as baseboards and under commodes in restrooms. The Quick Scrub has revolutionized the cleaning process by reaching all floor surfaces and eliminating the spread of dirt. This groundbreaking concept will gradually replace the standard cleaning method, mop bucket and wringer, that has been in use for over 130 years.

Another emerging trend is the demand for autonomous scrubbers. One company seized the opportunity by transforming a mid-size rider scrubber into an autonomous machine using their software and components. However, there are several important considerations when it comes to autonomous cleaning equipment, particularly safety. These machines rely on manual sweeping before scrubbing; if not done, it can lead to water being left behind. Additionally, objects can get caught in the squeegee, posing a risk of slip or fall accidents when no one is around. Furthermore, justifying the return on investment for autonomous scrubbers can be challenging, although pricing is gradually becoming more reasonable. While a few companies have taken early advantage of this market, others have invested significant amounts of money with little return. At our company, we are observing these developments and actively seeking to address the issues that plague autonomous scrubbers. Additionally, we are exploring other avenues to change the game in the cleaning industry.

I want to clarify that if I missed any of your innovations, please do not take offense. The following list represents the top contributions that I feel have significantly advanced the cleaning industry.

In summarizing how innovation sells in our industry, it is evident that each of these innovations improved features and capabilities to enhance functionality. They were designed to address specific needs and solve problems, ultimately providing users with superior experience. These innovations have helped individuals and businesses save time, effort, and resources.

Lessons Learned

- Innovation sells!
- Constantly monitor trends and anticipate shifts in needs as innovation is time sensitive.
- Explore other industries for innovative ideas to cross over and inspire innovation.
- An innovation should only be considered a true innovation if it fundamentally transforms a process.
- Be the pioneer, be the leader, and leave the rest behind!

CHAPTER 14

B2B

The cleaning industry has been significantly disrupted by various factors, and one of the key disruptions we will explore is the B2B sector.

B2B, which stands for Business-to-Business, has been around for many years. The concept of businesses selling products or services to other businesses has been in existence since the early days of commerce. However, with the advent of the Internet and e-commerce, B2B transactions have become more prevalent and efficient. Let's explore how B2B has revolutionized the procurement process and disrupted the cleaning industry's supply channel.

Digital marketplaces have emerged as game-changers, completely revolutionizing the way businesses connect and conduct transactions. However, it's important to note that the cleaning industry, with its unique complexities, still relies on cumbersome procurement processes and manual paperwork. While B2B companies offer customers the convenience of sourcing products, negotiating contracts, and managing supply chains with just a few clicks, it's important to recognize that the cleaning industry involves more than what online sources can fully comprehend. Labor costs make up a significant portion of the budget, and the total cost of a process is harder to visualize through a simple point-and-click interface. Additionally, location-specific cleaning problems often require hands-on solutions that cannot be easily addressed through digital platforms alone.

The streamlined nature of B2B commerce has indeed fostered greater transparency and accessibility, offering customers the ability to compare prices, evaluate product specifications, and read customer reviews with ease. This newfound transparency has the potential to empower customers to make more informed purchasing decisions. However, it is important to consider whether convenience alone is driving their buying choices, or if they are truly leveraging the available information.

Furthermore, the question arises as to whether this transparency has leveled the playing field, allowing smaller businesses to compete with larger enterprises. While it is true that digital platforms provide opportunities for smaller companies to showcase their offerings and reach a wider audience, there may still be challenges. The initial investment required to transition to digital platforms and adapt to new technologies can be a barrier for smaller businesses, potentially squeezing them out of the market.

In summary, while B2B commerce has brought about greater transparency and accessibility, it is essential to examine whether customers are making informed decisions or simply opting for convenience. Additionally, the impact on smaller businesses should be carefully considered, as the initial investment required to transition to digital platforms may pose challenges for their competitiveness in the market.

Let's examine a disrupter that has had a significant impact on the cleaning industry, Amazon.

In 1994, Amazon revolutionized the retail industry and caused significant disruption and opportunities for companies across various sectors. With its vast product selection, competitive pricing, and efficient delivery system, Amazon has become a dominant force in e-commerce and beyond.

One of the key disruptions caused by Amazon is the shift in consumer behavior. The convenience of online shopping and the wide range of products available on Amazon have led to a major competitor for the janitorial distribution trade. The instantaneous information that Amazon can provide the customer with a click is faster and more comprehensive than a salesperson can deliver on the street. Many companies have had to adapt their business models to compete with Amazon's online presence and provide unique value-added solutions.

Amazon has provided small and medium-sized businesses in the cleaning industry with opportunities to reach a wider customer base and compete with larger corporations. By listing their products on Amazon, these businesses can leverage the platform's vast customer reach and benefit from its reputation and trustworthiness.

The fulfillment by Amazon (FBA) program is particularly beneficial for these businesses. It allows them to outsource their storage, packaging, and shipping processes to Amazon. This not only reduces operational costs but also ensures fast and reliable delivery to customers. By utilizing FBA, businesses can focus on their core competencies while Amazon takes care of the logistics, providing a seamless and efficient fulfillment process.

However, it is important to note that by selling on Amazon, businesses are indeed transferring their potential customers to the Amazon platform. While this can provide immediate access to a large customer base, it also means that businesses are relying on Amazon's platform and infrastructure. This can create a dependency on Amazon and may limit direct customer relationships and control over the sales process.

Overall, Amazon's disruption in the cleaning industry has created both opportunities and challenges for small and medium-sized businesses. It has provided a platform for increased visibility and reach, as well as streamlined fulfillment processes. While the opportunities are abundant, the challenges of competing with Amazon's scale and efficiency should not be underestimated. Companies must continue to innovate and differentiate themselves to thrive in the evolving landscape of e-commerce.

B2B platforms have indeed facilitated seamless collaboration between suppliers and buyers. With direct lines of communication and the ability to share real-time information, companies can now establish stronger relationships and build long-term partnerships. This enhanced collaboration has resulted in improved supply chain management, reduced lead times, and increased overall operational efficiency, particularly in terms of soft cost savings.

It is important to recognize that there are limitations to the point-and-click nature of B2B platforms when it comes to location-specific problems. While operational efficiencies can be achieved through digital platforms, there are instances where a facility may encounter unique challenges that require a more consultative approach. In such cases, a simple point-and-click solution may not be sufficient to resolve the problem effectively. This is where the value of consultative expertise and personalized solutions comes into play, as they can provide the necessary insights and hands-on support to address location-specific issues.

The impact of B2B on the cleaning industry is undeniably significant. It has the potential to simplify and expedite the procurement process, but it is important to consider whether it has truly opened new doors for innovation or further commoditized the industry. On one hand, B2B platforms have expanded customers' options by allowing them to explore a wider range of suppliers, access a broader selection of products, and leverage certain technologies to optimize their operations. This can lead to increased efficiency and potentially cost savings.

However, it is important to also consider the potential drawbacks of relying solely on digital platforms. While B2B commerce offers convenience and accessibility, there is a risk of alienating the people who can provide valuable problem-solving expertise and deliver better outcomes. The cleaning industry often requires hands-on solutions and personalized approaches to address specific challenges. Overreliance on digital platforms may overlook the importance of human interaction and the consultative value that experienced professionals can bring to the table.

While B2B platforms have undoubtedly brought benefits to the cleaning industry by simplifying procurement and expanding options, it is important to strike a balance between the convenience of digital platforms and the value of human expertise. Embracing innovation while still recognizing the importance of personalized solutions can lead to the best solutions for customers in the cleaning industry.

The value of human expertise and hands-on solutions cannot be underestimated, as they play a vital role in delivering effective outcomes and ensuring customer satisfaction. Therefore, businesses in the cleaning industry should strive to strike a balance between leveraging digital advancements and utilizing the consultative support necessary to address unique challenges and provide optimal solutions.

B2B commerce has undoubtedly expanded the reach of companies, allowing them to transcend logistical borders and connect with suppliers through digital platforms. However, this has also sparked an ongoing debate about customer ownership, as businesses now find themselves competing with their own suppliers. In the janitorial supply industry, there is a unique challenge when it comes to B2B platforms-customers often have a strong desire to visualize product performance under real conditions before making a purchase. This raises the question of who will work with the customer to trial alternative ways for resolution and address their specific needs.

The disruption caused by B2B platforms extends beyond the initial order and into the replenishment phase. If customers are dissatisfied with the service provided by their current distributor, they can easily turn to online shopping to find the best price for replenishing the same branded product. This situation also exposes the risk of confrontational discussions regarding the initial pricing. To mitigate this issue, many manufacturers have implemented a minimum advertised price (MAP) policy to safeguard against such challenges for online buyers.

The janitorial industry generates a wealth of data through its transactions, providing businesses with valuable insights into market trends, customer behavior, and operational efficiency. However, many janitorial distributors struggle to effectively utilize this data to optimize strategies and maintain competitiveness. The power of data-driven decisions is now reshaping the cleaning industry, leading to changes in both the market and business practices.

To thrive in this evolving landscape, companies must transition from purely transactional approaches to a customer-centric mindset. By prioritizing a deep understanding of their customers' needs, pain points, and aspirations, businesses can deliver personalized experiences, tailored solutions, and exceptional customer service. This customer-centric approach has become a key differentiator for successful distribution companies, fueling growth and ensuring long-term success.

The shift towards data-driven decision-making and customer-centricity is not only a necessity but also an opportunity for janitorial distributors to thrive in the evolving market. By embracing these changes, businesses can unlock new avenues for growth, establish a competitive edge, and position themselves as industry leaders. This proactive approach allows companies to stay ahead of the curve, meet evolving customer needs, and drive long-term success in the janitorial industry.

Another example of a B2B business that changed an industry is Uber.

They revolutionized the transportation industry and caused significant disruption and transformation in how people move from one place to another. With its innovative ride-hailing platform and user-friendly mobile app, Uber has disrupted the traditional taxi industry and challenged the status quo of transportation.

One of the key disruptions caused by Uber is the democratization of transportation. By connecting riders directly with drivers through its app, Uber has provided a convenient and affordable alternative to traditional taxis. It has empowered individuals to become drivers and earn income on their own terms, creating new opportunities for entrepreneurship and flexible work arrangements.

Uber's disruptive model has also led to increased competition and improved customer experiences. Traditional taxi services have had to adapt and innovate to compete with Uber's convenience and transparency. Many taxi companies have developed their own ride-hailing apps and implemented dynamic pricing models to remain competitive in the market.

Uber's impact on the transportation market is undeniable, and it has paved the way for further innovation and disruption in the industry. The cost to deliver small orders in the janitorial supply industry is becoming increasingly scrutinized and deemed unprofitable. Uber has been expanding their portfolio of services. Could they be an option?

In the cleaning industry, customers still highly value the ability to witness tangible results at their location. This raises the question of whether the traditional brick-and-mortar supply model, which is currently prevalent, will eventually be replaced by regional distribution centers that can efficiently move inventories and achieve significant cost savings. By conducting business online, companies can reach a wider customer base without incurring additional costs associated with physical locations.

Let's examine a highly successful company that has disrupted the traditional brick-and- mortar model and has had a significant impact on janitorial and packaging in the industrial sector.

Uline operates primarily in the B2B sector, serving a wide range of industries, including manufacturing, retail, e-commerce, and more.

Uline's business model revolves around providing a comprehensive catalog of products and solutions for businesses' industrial supplies, including storage and organization solutions, safety equipment, and janitorial supplies.

One of the key aspects of Uline's business model is its extensive product inventory. The company boasts a vast selection of over 38,000 products, ensuring that customers can find everything they need in one place. Uline's catalog is available both online and in print, allowing customers to browse and order products through their preferred channel. They offer fast and reliable shipping, with multiple distribution centers strategically located across North America to ensure timely delivery.

Uline's success can be attributed to its commitment to quality and customer satisfaction. The company emphasizes the importance of delivering high-quality products and maintaining strong relationships with customers.

It is important to note that Uline is not a price cutting company. The customers pay extra for consistent on-time delivery, in many cases the next day. I recall designing an interactive worksheet for our sales force that integrated the janitorial pages from their catalog to demonstrate our price advantages and potential margin gains. It is shocking the quiet, yet huge impact they have made on the janitorial industry.

B2B platforms have intensified competition among distributors and manufacturers. With buyers having more options available to them, distributors must differentiate themselves by providing unique value-added services. It is important to thoroughly evaluate the total cost of the process, rather than solely focusing on price, as this can be a costly oversight, by offering comprehensive solutions and considering the overall value proposition.

While B2B platforms have proven effective in reducing the need for physical storefronts and sales teams in various industries, it is important to recognize that the cleaning industry revolves around labor savings, which typically accounts for 85-90 percent of the cleaning budget. Therefore, the presence of a professional value-added solutions provider remains crucial. Although advancements in AI technology may address the challenge of providing thought-provoking value online in the future, we will explore this in the next chapter.

Lessons Learned

- Disruptions usually center around efficiency gains. Embracing them can help you stay competitive and adapt to changing market dynamics.

- As a business owner, do you have the financial resources to invest in an e-commerce platform, or could you rely on your associations for support?

- Establishing a strong online presence with an online catalog and ordering system is essential for competing in the future.

- Adapt to e-commerce and embrace its benefits. It's equally important to recognize the value of personal interaction and the unique value proposition it brings.

- Leverage the strengths and contributions from each department in your organization; it will create a cohesive and agile approach to speed to market.

CHAPTER 15

THE EVOLUTION OF TECHNOLOGY

A s we envision the future, it's worth reflecting on the tools we relied on in the past. In the 1980s, when I began my business career, pagers, and personal digital assistants (PDAs) played a crucial role in staying informed and managing busy schedules. While I personally didn't use a pager, many sales representatives relied on them to receive notifications and then had to locate a payphone to contact the office and gather necessary information. I recall the day I replaced my daytime planner with my first PDA, which greatly enhanced my organization and productivity. Desktop computers were prevalent in businesses, running on the laborious DOS operating system. Fax machines were the primary means of transferring information during that era.

When I joined my first manufacturing company in 1987, I was tasked with the challenging responsibility of expanding the metropolitan New York territory. I remember carrying a significant number of coins with me, not just for transportation and other expenses associated with navigating the city, but also for using pay phones to conduct business. It's hard to imagine now, but in those days, one of my initial priorities was mapping out pay phones near my distribution partners, as communication and staying connected was key. These old pay phones didn't even accept credit cards, so if you didn't have enough change in your pocket, you were out of luck. I employed a similar strategy when corresponding with customers. I meticulously zoned in on locations of mailboxes, stocked up on stamps, and ensured they were all conveniently situated along my business route. I went through a significant number of stamps back then, as did many others who relied on US mail for their business communications.

In the late 1980s, I reached a point where I couldn't bear the inconvenience anymore, and that's when car phones were introduced. I use the term "car phone" deliberately because they were so large that they could only be installed in cars. Outside of the car, they resembled miniature pieces of luggage. I was incredibly proud of my investment and eagerly shared my new phone number with everyone. However, my excitement quickly turned to dismay when Brenda received the first car phone bill, totaling a staggering $881.00. I'll never forget my reaction. I calmly told her that it was simply a cost of doing business, but deep down, I knew I had to find ways to cut expenses elsewhere. The pace of business was astonishing. While I do miss the old pay phones, I also remember the frustration of waiting in line, especially during the cold winter months. Another valuable tool that emerged in the 1980s was voicemail. Prior to its introduction, if you couldn't reach someone directly, you had to rely on a receptionist to take a message, transcribe it by hand, and pass it along to the intended recipient. I often wonder where all the receptionists have gone. They were truly invaluable during those days.

In the early 1990s, I recall purchasing my first laptop loaded with Windows 3.0. Although it was a bit bulky, it served its purpose well. I began developing spreadsheets alongside a close, long-time friend, David, and others in the industry, fascinated by how we could justify a sale by considering all the components involved in a product or service. We expanded our focus beyond just equipment and started incorporating everything related to the cleaning industry. It was an exciting time that sparked our imagination. Some individuals like David eventually found their calling in the consulting business and made significant contributions to the cleaning industry.

It feels like a dream-where did all the pay phones and mailboxes go? In the late 1990s, the World Wide Web became widely accessible, revolutionizing communication and information sharing. Email quickly became the primary mode of communication, replacing traditional mail for many business purposes. The ability to send a message without leaving a voicemail was unheard of before. These tools made communication fast and easy, accelerating business activities and contributing to a vibrant economy. Laptops enabled sales professionals to work remotely, and I still remember the old camera-in-a-box I used to capture before and after pictures, always emphasizing the measurable outcomes. I invested in expensive cameras and the old JVC video recorders. If you thought my first car phone was big, you should have seen that one. I always sought tools that would make my sales process quicker, more convincing, and supported by visual content. As they say, a picture is worth a thousand words.

The 2000s brought about smartphones with built-in cameras, rendering many of my previous tool investments obsolete. Looking back, it's remarkable how technology gradually made these trusted business tools vanish. I can't even begin to count the number of business VHS tapes I have stored in the attic. This was also the era when social media started gaining prominence, allowing us to communicate, promote, and network on a broader scale.

In the mid-to-late 2000s, we witnessed the emergence of lighter and more portable devices, along with the advent of virtual meetings and video conferencing. I can only imagine how much more I could have achieved in sales if I had had access to video conferencing capabilities.

What lies ahead? Technology is advancing at an unprecedented pace. There are several areas that I believe will enhance your selling skills and income potential. Artificial intelligence (AI) and the Internet of Things (IoT) have emerged as competing technologies, but they hold the potential to provide a wealth of information that can level the playing field for sales representatives, provided they embrace these technologies and utilize them as tools in their sales toolbox. Let's look at what's happening today.

Tools of the Present and Near Future

Advanced data analytics techniques can predict customer behavior, identify potential leads, and optimize sales strategies based on historical data and patterns. This leads me to wonder, what lies beyond CRM systems? Could pipeline data eventually be transformed into an order without the need for human representation? Will these advanced data systems render salespeople obsolete? Will the sales process shift more towards analytics and away from personal relationships? It's important to note that the cleaning industry is complex, and achieving labor reductions requires personalized approaches to measure outcomes and savings. Therefore, these advanced analytics should be embraced, especially if they can provide insights into predicting the behaviors of both existing and potential clients.

Advanced automation tools have the potential to streamline sales processes, automate repetitive tasks, and provide sales teams with more efficient workflows. The focus will be on how to accelerate the sales process. Online ordering systems will become the standard, rendering traditional methods such as fax and email obsolete, much like pay phones and mailboxes. Electronic transfer of funds (ETF) will be seamlessly integrated into the system, creating a closed loop electronically. These advancements will not only revolutionize collections but also streamline order processing. Salespeople will have more time to dedicate to meeting customer needs on-site. In the future, successful salespeople will possess a deep understanding of their customers' operations, positioning themselves as trusted advisors and integral members of their customers' cost reduction initiatives.

Mobile apps and tools will empower sales representatives to access customer information, product details, training, and sales collateral on-the-go, enhancing productivity and responsiveness. However, the effectiveness of mobile apps will depend on their level of interactivity. If they merely serve as information repositories, they may become outdated with the emergence of AI. In the cleaning industry, I anticipate a gradual adoption of mobile apps or just a leapfrog to AI. Industry tends to be cautious in accepting and implementing new technologies, preferring to take measured steps forward.

The advancements in social media platforms and tools have empowered sales professionals to engage with prospects, build relationships, and utilize social networks for lead generation and sales conversions. I believe that social media has the potential to go even further and become a direct conduit to sales. This is just my personal speculation and vision. Imagine meeting a business client on social media and fast tracking the conversion into a sale during the initial meet and greet. Could social media be the future platform that accelerates the sales process and generates speedy returns? It is possible that cleaning products are already being sold on a social media platform.

Emerging Methods to Help You Sell

The advancement that I believe has the biggest potential to make a significant impact on our cleaning industry is artificial intelligence (AI). AI-powered sales assistants can analyze customer data, offer personalized recommendations, and assist sales representatives in their interactions with customers. Rather than being intimidating, this technology should be embraced. It can help sales professionals become more responsive to their customers and provide valuable information in real-time. Keep in mind the cleaning industry has a huge population of highly experienced salespeople retiring. Will that intellectual property be passed on or lost? Could AI be the answer? In the past, we have tried to share valuable information to secure business opportunities. However, it's important to remember that if you're not utilizing an AI tool, someone else will be. The only concern I have is regarding the gathering of information on the backend and how that personalized data will be used in the future. It's important to ensure that the use of this information remains ethical and respects client privacy.

Virtual reality (VR) and augmented reality (AR) are immersive technologies that have the potential to revolutionize the customer experience by enabling virtual product demonstrations, interactive sales presentations, and virtual showrooms. At my company, we firmly believe in the power of this technology, and we are excited about the advancements we will be introducing in this area. Interactive sales presentations and virtual showrooms will soon become the norm in the cleaning industry. While product demonstrations in a virtual environment can be informative, it is important to acknowledge that the unique characteristics of each customer's facility may not be fully captured. While the fundamental functions of the products can be showcased, most customers will still want to see how the product performs in their specific facility, under their unique conditions, and with their employees before making a purchase decision.

Customers will explore virtual stores and examine products from the convenience of their office, immersing themselves in an interactive experience. They will utilize this experience as an educational tool to evaluate potential partners and determine with whom they feel comfortable meeting to discuss partnerships. This virtual exploration will serve as an interview process, replacing the need for personal communication in the initial stages of the buyer's journey.

AI-powered shopping assistants have the capability to analyze customer preferences, browsing history, and social media data to provide personalized product recommendations and assist with purchasing decisions. While this may seem intimidating, it is already a reality. Can AI effectively select the right product or solution for a cleaning job? Could AI potentially replace the role of the buyer and seller? In our complex industry, I would argue that AI alone cannot fully address the intricacies involved. However, in less complex industries, the impact of AI could escalate rapidly.

Furthermore, customers can now utilize VR technology to visualize products in their own environment before making a purchase, enabling them to see how items fit or look in real-time. If we reach a point where this technology becomes widespread, salespeople will face intense competition. While I do not foresee this technology being widely adopted in our industry for some time, it is important to remember how quickly things can change, just like the disappearance of pay phones.

The increasing popularity of smart speakers and voice assistants has made it possible for customers to make purchases through simple voice commands, offering a more convenient and hands-free buying experience. Online buying formats will soon become more voice-activated, speeding up the interactive process and providing tracking capabilities to identify any mistakes made by the buyer or seller.

Social media platforms, I believe, will continue to evolve into shopping destinations, allowing users to discover and directly purchase products within their favorite social apps. It is important to know whether your current customers are active on social media. If your company is not currently active on social media, it is important to reassess your position on the matter and get connected.

More businesses in the future will adopt subscription-based models, providing customers with regular product deliveries or access to exclusive services, thereby creating a recurring revenue stream. This shift will not only impact the selling process but also the structure of sales compensation programs. It is important to note that subscriptions should be approached with caution, as they can end up costing more over the term of the investment. Subscriptions tend to lean towards flexibility, with new units or technological advancements introduced to the market, ensuring that customers always have access to the latest technology.

As consumer awareness and concern for sustainable products continue to grow, the market will witness a rise in eco-friendly and socially responsible brands. Companies that align with these values will gain a competitive advantage in the future. We have all witnessed the movement towards safer and healthier buildings. There may be technological advancements that measure the health and safety of buildings. . . It's already happening with smart buildings. If you are unable to offer a sustainable solution, you risk being left behind. Customers will increasingly demand sustainability, and as a professional salesperson, it is imperative to be prepared to offer sustainable solutions, learn quickly about these evolving technological advances, and take a proactive position to offer solutions.

These emerging trends in buying and selling reflect the evolving landscape of commerce, driven by technological advancements, shifting consumer preferences, and a focus on convenience, personalization, and sustainability. Embracing these trends will enable cleaning businesses to stay ahead and thrive in the future market.

Lessons Learned

- Visualize the rapid pace of technology and stay ahead of the curve.
- Embrace technology early on, or you will be fundamentally inadequate.

- Invest in emerging technology or you will be left behind.
- AI is a friend of the professional salesperson, not a replacement.
- VR can and will emerge to speed up the sales.

CHAPTER 16

BREAKING WAVES

In the realm of sales, success hinges on the ability to cultivate enduring relationships, comprehend customer needs, and deliver value. A proficient salesperson possesses a distinctive skill set and a range of qualities that distinguishes them from their peers.

Reflecting on my differentiating traits, I have ingrained the habit of actively listening to customers, identifying their pain points, tailoring my value proposition to their requirements, and establishing a foundation of trust that positions me as a trusted advisor. This breakthrough occurred during my initial sales role calling on Ciba-Geigy in the early '80s, leaving an indelible impression on my career. I encourage readers to delve into their own sales experiences and uncover the structured framework that paved the way for their future triumphs. Have you built upon it? Personally, I frequently revisit this experience, constantly analyzing what transpired and contemplating ways to enhance it further. I meticulously compiled a list of customer pain points throughout my career, crafted compelling value propositions, and fostered trust with every individual that I met.

A portion of my drive and determination stems from my involvement in competitive sports. I possess a burning desire to outperform the competition every day. If ever there is doubt regarding my passion for victory, one need only recall my unwavering determination to attend that meeting in Toledo, where I drove tirelessly throughout the night. I refused to be denied. In the sales profession, competitiveness is a prerequisite; it is an industry that thrives on competition. Personally, my focus is solely on winning and losing. I gauge my success daily, not monthly, quarterly, or annually. Each day presents an opportunity for triumph, and if I encounter setbacks, I strategize in the evening to make amends the following day. Some may perceive this as placing excessive pressure on oneself, but throughout my career, I have consistently thrived under self-imposed pressure.

Successful salespeople understand that empathy is important for building strong relationships. In the cleaning industry, which heavily relies on relationships, this principle remains unchanged, at least for the foreseeable future. Throughout my career, I have always prioritized helping others, regardless of any time constraints. By placing others before myself, I knew that the benefits would eventually come back to me. In a way, I have been paying it forward since the beginning of my business journey. Some individuals in the industry may question why I am writing a book, but the truth is that sharing real-life selling experiences can greatly assist others in their own careers. I am committed to paying it forward until I am no longer physically or emotionally capable. Networking has been a part of my life for a long time, and I have found that the most impactful connections were often unrelated to what I was selling. Selling can be a simple and rewarding profession if you choose to prioritize your customers over your commission. This lesson became evident to me quickly in the fast-paced business environment of Manhattan, which resembled playing high-tempo basketball. I realized that by helping my customers make a significant profit, they would reciprocate and contribute to my success. Once again, I placed the customers' needs ahead of my own financial gain. Through my strong work ethic and unwavering desire to succeed, I surpassed my competition. By building trust with your customers and ensuring their success every day, you will be amazed at how readily they welcome you into their team.

A successful salesperson understands the importance of investing time and effort into thoroughly understanding their product or service. Personally, I always made it a priority to familiarize myself with every aspect of what I was selling. I would mentally rehearse potential obstacles that could arise during the sales process and ensure that I was well-prepared for each sales call. However, I am unsure of how much time other professional salespeople dedicate to preparation. By preparation, I am not referring to simply gathering support documents and data, but rather taking the time to truly understand the potential customer's business. If possible, I would even visit their facility to gain a deeper understanding. It is important not to use lack of access as an excuse to neglect learning about their pain points. In fact, some of these pain points may come up during the initial conversation, and if they don't, the customer may not be interested in meeting with you in the first place. As a salesperson, it is important to exceed the customer's expectations and be prepared to fast-track the sales process. I can recall numerous instances where customers were impressed by my knowledge of their pain points and how I systematically addressed them. I have never had a customer question or been upset by my level of preparation. Salespeople must recognize that customers are also preparing for meetings and may be more knowledgeable than expected due to advancements in technology. Therefore, it is key for salespeople to be prepared for a fast-paced sales process. Another practice I have found effective is requesting a tour of the customer's facility. This allows me to gauge their pride in their facilities and assess the level of comfort they have in building a business case. If they decline to give a tour, it could indicate a lack of trust or discomfort with the condition of their facility. By conducting a brief site visit prior to the meeting, you can proactively address any obvious issues they may be experiencing. Throughout my career, regardless of my position, I have found that preparation is the key to success. Unfortunately, many people do not allocate enough time to adequately prepare for sales. Imagine how a competitive sports team would fare if they neglected to review game films, scout their opponents, or practice game-ready plays. Their chances of winning would be drastically reduced. I have always prioritized playing the percentages. I developed a simple formula divided into categories, each involving preparation, and weighed them according to overall success. Before making a sales call, I would run through this exercise to ensure I had covered all necessary aspects. If I skipped any step, I knew my percentages of success would be diminished. This approach forced me to be prepared and increased my chances of success. As salespeople, we all have numerous tasks and responsibilities, but nothing is more important than dedicating time to prepare.

Sales is undoubtedly a challenging and demanding field, but successful salespeople possess an unwavering resilience. To win, you must be willing to experience losses and feel the pain that comes with them. One example from my own experience, which was detailed in an earlier chapter, was when I lost a national account. It wasn't due to lack of preparation; there were external factors beyond my control. Even after thirty years, the memory of that loss still stings. However, it served as a driving force for me to become better. Looking back, I am grateful for that loss because it fueled my determination to succeed. Rejection, setbacks, and failure can be beneficial if you take the time to learn from them. Unfortunately, many salespeople neglect to debrief themselves after a failed call. By reflecting on and analyzing those experiences, you can adapt and make the necessary changes to achieve victory. On the other hand, if you don't take the time to learn from your failures, it becomes a detrimental habit that is difficult to break. Ultimately, this hinders your potential as a professional salesperson and prevents you from reaching your highest level of success.

A successful salesperson recognizes the significance of hard work and discipline. It's important to acknowledge that selling is a profession, and as a professional salesperson, you are compensated based on your performance. Just as a sports figure would say they are a professional basketball player, you should proudly identify yourself as a professional salesperson. Unfortunately, many people tend to underestimate the value of this profession. However, it is important to remember that businesses rely on salespeople for their survival. Just imagine a world without salespeople in the '80s and '90s-companies would have struggled to survive. Therefore, it is essential to take pride in your profession. Sales is an individualized profession, like playing tennis. Your success or failure is determined by your strategic approach and your ability to be proactive and anticipate.

Throughout my career of working for companies, as well as owning my own, I have come to understand the importance of teamwork. In successful companies, the team factor is always front and center, and all members share in the accolades. No individual team member is more important than the others. It is advantageous to operate in parallel with one another to achieve victory. By building a strong team to support one another's strengths and weaknesses, everyone becomes more engaged and appreciates the support.

The sales landscape is constantly evolving, and successful salespeople understand the importance of embracing change. I am not alone in this experience, as many of us have had to adapt throughout our careers. We have witnessed the disappearance of pay phones, mailboxes, daytimers, and notepads. I remember starting to build ROIs and spreadsheets back in the late '80s, embracing technology and adopting a pay-forward mentality with my business associates. Although these sheets had little to do with my current profession, we were open to learning new techniques, technologies, and strategies to stay ahead of the curve. My recommendation is to explore how new technologies can assist you in helping your customers. It is important to stay informed and avoid a situation where your customers know more about your products and services than you do. Once that happens, your relevance diminishes. In the cleaning industry, for example, the Internet has provided customers with accessible information to aid their buying decisions. To exceed the evolving needs of your customers, it is essential to adapt and leverage emerging tools and platforms that enhance the customer experience. Always be smarter than your customer.

Becoming a successful professional salesperson requires a choice: do you want to be a wave rider or a wave breaker? I came up with this analogy when I was young, sitting by the shore and observing a rough surf. Living near the beach after my father retired, I had the opportunity to witness surfers taking full advantage of the high waves. Some would paddle out, putting in the hard work to enjoy the ride back in. Others would receive assistance from small boats to position themselves for the waves. It made me reflect on the personal gratification one would experience by choosing the harder path, rather than relying on help without fully appreciating the effort required to get there. From that day forward, I began looking at life and business from that perspective. To break waves, you must be willing to put in the effort and take risks. You need to build your business through hard work and create a lasting impact for others even when you're no longer around. This is what building a legacy is all about. On the other hand, wave riders go through life seeking the easy road, benefiting from someone else's hard work and dedication. By choosing to break waves, you will reach your highest potential as a professional salesperson.

Break some waves!

ACKNOWLEDGMENTS

I am deeply grateful to my wife Brenda, my children Meaghann and Connor, friends, and colleagues who have played a significant role in the creation of this book.

I want to express my heartfelt appreciation to the team at Canoe Tree Press: Gordon McClellan, the publisher; Suanne Laqueur, the production coordinator; Libby Bell, the project coordinator; Chris Dorning, the cover designer; and Aiden Angeli, the graphics designer. Their support and dedication have been invaluable in bringing this project to fruition and allowing me to share my experiences and knowledge.

I am grateful to my mentors, Charlie Hasper, Ames Shuel, and Larry Hines, whose business acumen and friendship have shaped my career in profound ways. I feel fortunate to have had the opportunity to learn from these industry leaders.

A special mention goes to Camila Salazar, a dear friend who provided valuable input on the book's structure. Your inspiration and guidance have been instrumental, and I am truly grateful.

Lastly, I offer my deepest gratitude to the Lord Jesus. Your presence has been a constant source of strength and guidance throughout my career, health challenges, and aspirations for the future. Thank you for your unwavering support.

ABOUT THE AUTHOR

Bill Fisher has dedicated forty-two years of his professional career to the sanitary maintenance industry. He kickstarted his professional journey after graduating from Mississippi State University, where he also played basketball for the SEC Bulldogs. Beginning as a sales representative and sales manager for Sanitary Supply Specialties (SSS) in South Jersey, he spent seven years honing his skills. Bill then transitioned to Windsor Industries, where he held various positions including NY district manager, national accounts manager, national sales manager, and VP of sales.

Seeking new challenges, Bill moved to Indiana to assume the role of executive vice president for HP Products. Driven by his ambition to lead a company by the age of forty, he accepted the position of president at Pacific Floorcare in Muskegon, Michigan. After eight successful years with Pacific, Bill returned to Indiana to establish his own company, Intelligent Cleaning Systems. Under his leadership, the company experienced rapid growth, eventually leading to its acquisition by Flex Pac, a prominent packaging company. Bill played a pivotal role in developing Flex Pac's facilities division as vice president of facility solutions for five years. Currently, he has rejoined Pacific Floorcare as their president.

Outside of his professional endeavors, Bill has been married to his wife, Brenda, for thirty-eight years. They have two children: Connor, who served in the army for eight years and is entering the world of cyber security, and Meaghann, an executive account manager for an AI company, and the new addition granddaughter, Eleonore.

Ringing the bell: last radiation treatment

www.ingramcontent.com/pod-product-compliance
Lightning Source LLC
Chambersburg PA
CBHW021716120626
46545CB00004B/1588